No.thing

Leverage Your "Nothing" by
Leaping into God's Everything

ESTHER PANNEBAKER

HIGH BRIDGE BOOKS
HOUSTON

No.thing
by Esther Pannebaker

Copyright © 2021 by Esther Pannebaker

All rights reserved.

Printed in the United States of America
ISBN: 978-1-954943-15-5

Scripture quotations marked CSB are from The Christian Standard Bible. Copyright © 2017 by Holman Bible Publishers. Used by permission. Christian Standard Bible®, and CSB® are federally registered trademarks of Holman Bible Publishers, all rights reserved.

Scripture quotations marked NLT are from the Holy Bible, New Living Translation, copyright © 1996, 2004, 2015 by Tyndale House Foundation. Used by permission of Tyndale House Publishers, Inc., Carol Stream, Illinois 60188. All rights reserved.

Scripture quotations marked ICB are from the International Children's Bible®. Copyright © 1986, 1988, 1999 by Thomas Nelson, Inc. Used by permission. All rights reserved.

Scripture quotations marked VOICE are from The Voice™. Copyright © 2008 by Ecclesia Bible Society. Used by permission. All rights reserved.

Scripture quotations marked ESV are from the ESV® Bible (The Holy Bible, English Standard Version®), copyright © 2001 by Crossway Bibles, a publishing ministry of Good News Publishers. Used byvpermission. All rights reserved.

Scripture quotations marked NIV are from THE HOLY BIBLE, NEW INTERNATIONAL VERSION®, NIV® Copyright © 1973, 1978, 1984, 2011 by Biblica, Inc.® Used by permission. All rights reserved worldwide.

Scripture quotations marked TPT are from The Passion Translation®. Copyright © 2017, 2018, 2020 by Passion & Fire Ministries, Inc. Used by permission. All rights reserved. ThePassionTranslation.com.

High Bridge Books titles may be purchased in bulk for educational, business, fundraising, or sales promotional use. For information, please contact High Bridge Books via www.HighBridgeBooks.com/contact.

Photography by Heather McKinney with HM Photography & Boutique, LLC.
Book cover design by Felicity Bridges with Signarama.

Published in Houston, Texas, by High Bridge Books.

Contents

Foreword _____ v

Introduction _____ vii

Section One | Now thing_____ 1

  1. Now What?_____ 3

  2. Not. a. Thing Looks Like I Thought It Would _____ 11

  3. Please God ... Do Something!_____ 19

  4. And YOU ... Have Done Nothing! _____ 27

  5. The Divine Fermata! _____ 37

Section Two | Next thing _____ 45

  6. The Shift _____ 47

  7 Reframe and Rename _____ 53

  8. Pull Out the Cotton Balls _____ 63

  9. Set Down Your Water Pot_____ 71

  10. Googling ... but Nothing Helpful Pops Up _____ 79

Section Three | New thing _____ 85

  11. Breaking Free _____ 87

  12. Nothing Wrong with Nothing_____ 95

  13. You Ain't Seen Nothing Yet!_____ 101

  14. Grit, Spit, & Grin_____ 107

  15. Bigger Beards and Bushy Brows_____ 113

Section Four | Know thing _____ 121

    16. Why Nothing? _____ 123

    17. Not for Nothing_____ 129

    18. Nothing Wasted_____ 135

    19. A Bigger Small _____ 145

    20. All or Nothing _____ 151

Afterword _____ 157

Notes _____ 161

Foreword

Esther Pannebaker has the true gift of preparing a table. When she invites people into her home, they feel loved, honored, and understood. There is laughter and sometimes tears, and everyone leaves a little lighter and a little more inspired to do better. Somehow, Esther has found a way to put her gift into words. This book will welcome you like a well-set table, provide you with the nourishment you didn't even know you needed, and leave you wanting to be more like Jesus. I'm sure that there will also be plenty of laughs and tears and soul searching along the way.

For the past six years, the Pannebaker family has been an anchor in our community. They lead from whatever seat they occupy. Esther has leaned into so many gaps and continues to work relentlessly to show the light of Christ to those around her. Some people talk a good game, Esther lives her walk with Jesus out every single day in every situation. One of my favorite things about her is her gut-level honesty. She is always kind and positive but also 100% honest. That makes her stories of faith and struggle and triumph so incredibly relatable and authentic. You are not reading a polished version of Esther. You are reading the amazing woman that we as a community have had the privilege to serve alongside for so many years.

As you read this book, I want to encourage you to stop and ponder after each chapter some important questions. First, what am I learning? Becoming aware of new information or being reminded of a familiar truth is part of the change cycle. Acknowledge what you are learning and write it down. Second, ask yourself what this information is asking you to evaluate.

Every learned truth should cause us to evaluate our lives. It is like a new lens exposing new truth about ourselves, our lives, and our relationships. Finally, how can I put this truth into action? One small step is enough.

I know you will enjoy learning from, laughing with, and getting to know Esther in the pages of *No.thing*. You are fortunate to be sitting at this table, and I know it will be a life-changing experience.

—Pastor Phillip Deas
  Lead pastor, Northpoint Community Church
  John Maxwell certified coach

Introduction

/No.thing/ n.

1. *A period when things feel hopeless or hard.*
2. *A no or wait circumstance that positions one for the thing God has for them.*

NOTHING. It's a word we dislike. In fact, we hate it! Nothing for dinner. Nothing to wear. Nothing in the mail. Nothing in the bank. Nothing on the calendar. "No" seems cruel when we are expecting the "thing" to show up in our lives. We seem to cycle through no *things* of life, regardless of our age.

In our teen years, we see no *thing* in our future. In college, we stress over no *thing* on our finger. Marriage many times produces no *thing* in the womb. In mid-life, our kids leave the house and we are once again faced with no *thing* left in the nest.

No *thing* is a problem! So how do we deal with a nothing situation? Do we look around and ask, *Is there more to life?* Maybe we eventually find ourselves either excusing the no *thing* or hiding it. Here's the deal—not only do we despise nothings, but we also don't know what to do with them.

We are afraid of nothings! Do you know why? It's because we cannot get a handle on a no *thing*. We cannot explain the nothingness we feel and the nothing we see (or don't see). We question: if God is really for us, then why do we still have no *thing*?

Living in a society searching for fullness, we have the God-given answers at our fingertips, yet sometimes we, too, fight feelings of guilt while we are running, drained both emotionally and spiritually. Unmet expectations leave us with empty dreams, empty arms, and empty hearts. We may even feel alone and start asking ourselves if this is the way the rest of life will be.

You might have secretly wondered if *No.things* are actually normal for Christians. As you've found yourself waiting between a no and the thing God is doing. All the while, you desperately long for a life filled with purpose and destiny—one that isn't empty, deprived, or wasted.

What if I told you that your *no* or your period of *wait* (.) was taking you to the *thing* God has for you?

The enemy doesn't want you to know this, but it's true. The Bible is full of *No.things*, and they do not scare God at all. In Genesis, we learn that He created the world from nothing, and Job 26:7 tells us, "He hung the earth upon nothing." Satan tries to fool us into thinking that God has left us when we don't see anything happening or feel anything moving. In fact, He knows exactly what to do with our lacks and uses *No.thing* to bring us into the thing He has prepared for us.

What does nothing look like for you? Maybe it involves a lost job, a misplaced identity, or missed opportunity. Possibly your nothing is a distant wayward child or a nearly extinct relationship that is causing a void in your life. Do you feel like you're in a wasted season or a weird situation? Is there an unanswered prayer or unrevealed promise just within reach, but you need a friend with an encouraging word or a boost in the right direction? I'll start by telling you part of my story if you promise to join me. Let's do this together, shall we?

Section One

Now thing

1

Now What?

The pessimist sees difficulty in every opportunity. The optimist sees opportunity in every difficulty.

—Winston Churchill

Most of us endured living in the "now" in the spring of 2020, when COVID-19 swept over the entire world and showed up in our modern-day civilization. It wasn't some ancient pandemic we read about in a textbook. We were living it.

Quarantine sidelined us for multiple weeks with life that was uncertain, unscheduled, and unprecedented for most of our known world. Systems and structures groaned under the pressure, as none of us was ready for a pandemic to strike the land. (Who ever thought toilet paper and Lysol would be the most coveted items hoarded and sold for mega bucks on eBay?) Weeks turned into months of "house arrest," and plans on our calendars crumbled like air castles while everything we knew was stripped away.

We began to use terms like "essential," "social distancing," and "COVID jail." Cities that never sleep were oddly quiet. Arenas, concert halls, churches, schools, and stadiums became stilled. And while the church buildings were empty, the hearts of the real body of Christ became full, brimming to life under the pressure. As the silence beckoned us to reflect upon what mattered most, we realized that nothing but Jesus really mattered anyway.

No.thing puts us in a different mindset—one without distraction where we catch sight of a new perspective and gain clarity for the next thing God will work out through the difficult season. Rarely do we learn from our success, but when we discover the silver lining inside of our trouble, new things begin to emerge.

The apostle James has some things to say about this. In his epistle, he double-dares us to face our reality with confidence: "When troubles of any kind come your way, consider it an opportunity for great joy. For you know that when your faith is tested, your endurance has a chance to grow. So let it grow, for when your endurance is fully developed, you will be perfect and complete, needing *nothing*" (Jas. 1:2-4 NLT, emphasis mine). James was challenging the early Christian church, dispersed throughout the land and facing extreme adversity, to count it all joy when trials came their way, knowing that God was working great things within them. But how did they do this? And today, how do we?

Overcoming the Reality Barrier

The first thing we have to do in overcoming *No.thing* is to choose to confront reality rather than to ignore it. On multiple occasions, I've tried brushing adversity off with, "Oh, it's nothing …" But you know as well as I do that the noes and waits of unrealized dreams, unmet desires, and unfulfilled plans rock our world. I've cycled too many times through these formidable thoughts of being "stuck," "stripped," or "stagnant."

Admiral James Stockdale was a United States military officer, held captive for eight years during the Vietnam War. Being tortured repeatedly by his captors gave him no reason to believe he would survive prison camp, much less be able to someday return home to his wife.

Yet Stockdale held on to seemingly impossible faith, even in the unknowable. Curiously, the defining advantage that brought him out alive and safely home was different than most of his optimistic cell mates—those who thought they would be out by Easter or by Christmas but suffered mentally and emotionally as yet another year passed while remaining in captivity. The disappoint-

> *To both keep our sanity and find our solution, we have to first clearly identify the source of our No.thing and intentionally confront it with a solid belief in God's everything.*

ment that met their optimism year after year of imprisonment finally overpowered them, and as Stockdale noted, "They died of a broken heart."

When they were forced to face reality, it all became overwhelming and too much to handle. In a trying situation, sheer optimism wasn't enough. So what was the difference-maker for Stockdale? Simply this: he was not afraid to mentally confront the reality of the severity of his situation. He owned it yet retained faith that he would prevail in the end. From his experience, the term The Stockdale Paradox was coined.[1]

In his book, *Good to Great*, researcher and consultant Jim Collins quantifies the topic of overcoming difficult situations with the following quote from his interview with Admiral Stockdale:

> You must retain faith that you will prevail in the end, regardless of the difficulties. And, at the same time … confront the most brutal facts of your current reality, whatever they may be.

I cried when I read this story, as I can relate to the gravity of emotional captivity. This empowering act of confronting reality is key to our mental and emotional health. To both keep our sanity and find our solution, we have to first clearly identify the source of our *No.thing* and intentionally confront it with a solid belief in God's everything. By considering opposition as an opportunity for joy and growth in our lives, we gain a foothold when we feel like we are at a standstill.

No.thing requires us to grab hold of more than optimistic faith. We need "impossible faith" grounded in a God who has big answers for us. True joy is found in trusting God when we are stuck in a rut and not a thing looks like we thought it would. I'm not asking you to negate your adverse situation, but when we quit wrestling with *No.thing* and start dealing with the now thing directly in front of us, we discover more than enough strength to fully embrace the next thing God is preparing! "Nothing is impossible with God" (Luke 1:37 NLT) literally means He is incapable of doing nothing. He is working and never stops, even when we can't see it! Do you believe it?

If we hope to go forward and upward, we can't afford to let the negativity of a *No.thing* sneak into our inmost beings unchecked; if we do, it will inevitably rob our hope and smother our joy. I refuse to let this happen to you, because it almost destroyed me.

Discovering More Than a "No"

My *No.thing* journey began in 2005, when our 10-year-old daughter was pre-diagnosed with a brain tumor. As we sat in the exam room, the doctor explained that her eyes were crossing due to extreme pressure on her optic nerve. The blunt truth was revealed—she needed more than glasses. He described what appeared to be a large mass located directly between her eyes in the middle of her forehead. He gave us a whirl of details on success rates at Mayo Clinic and of children's brain surgeries. He then slowly reached for our hands and asked if we would like to pray.

Like a tsunami, that day spun my world around and set me on an extended path of noes and waits that resembled huge crashing waves. They would force me to trust God in a way I had never before experienced. Ultimately, I would learn to trust that the thing He brings me into is the very thing He wants to bring me through. But on that day, in that year, and within that space, I could think of 100 other ways for God to grow me. At the time, I wasn't asking for a no; neither did I desire to wait. I expected a thing—a certain thing—to be my answer, but His answers were nothing like mine. *That is true of most of us, we won't to tell God what we need,*

I really didn't want to open up and tell you (or anyone) about the insecurity I felt or the gaps I discovered within myself during this journey. Not really. It forces me to reveal the rawness of my humanity and the deficit of my thinking—the very place of deciding that a "thing" would fix me.

In retrospect, I can see His perfect plan inside the realities of *No.thing*. It made me a better person and quite literally changed my life by challenging me to exchange my internal will for His eternal way.

I'll fully explain what I mean by *No.thing* in the next few chapters, but first, I want you to know my heart. I've been through several seasons where it looked like a definite *no* and felt like an eternal *wait*, so I get it. I am not speaking down to you. I am *with* you. And spoiler alert, I am still going through seasons of *No.things*, but with God's help, I'm getting stronger and wiser and He's enabling me to walk with peace through each situation. It's a big deal because I have exchanged coping and surviving for hoping and thriving. This girl is no longer stuck; she will soar! And so will you. It starts with taking small mental steps from where we are now to where we hope to be in the future.

First, we must learn to *confront* the adverse feelings of *no* and *wait* by accepting our situation for what it currently is.

Second, *consider* the trouble of our *no* and *wait* as an opportunity granted to us for gaining great joy.

Finally, admit that we have been given an incredible *chance* to grow in faith by enduring the hardship of a *no* and *wait*.

Open Up

Moment of truth. Let it all out. Write it at the bottom of this page. Pencil it. I don't care—sharpie it! What is the *thing* you so desperately desire, pray over, and long for? That thing so close to your heart that you take to work, to church, and to bed with you. Could it be an event that just hasn't happened yet, a change that hasn't quite materialized? Maybe the *thing* involves other people whose decisions affect you as well. They really don't seem to get it, and you wonder if they ever will. Does the *no* seem to be getting louder and the *wait* longer? Are you at a point in your marriage or ministry where things appear to be empty or over? Have your circumstances left you feeling like it may be your fault and that possibly even *you* are a nothing?

I encourage you to begin releasing pent up tension by jotting down some things you would like to see God working out in your life throughout the coming months. Start by answering the questions that I just posed—a personalized prayer list of sorts—one you can come back to reflect upon as you read this book.

Next, in your own handwriting, jot James 1:2-4 at the bottom of your page. Let the words sink into your heart. Finally, I want you to pray over the items you listed. Prayer is simply the desire of your heart put into words. I've provided lines throughout this book for you to journal your thoughts and prayers. I believe you will celebrate victories as we continue. Go ahead, bow your head wherever you are, and ask God to meet you exactly in the middle of your *No.thing*.

Louie's

Digging Deeper Prayer

Dear Heavenly Father,

I come to You with an open but heavy heart. I have so many un-answered questions that I lay before you. Will you open my eyes to see your ways, my heart to receive your truths, and my mind to understand those things that you have waiting for me? I'm upgrading my *No*, God, in exchange for your *Yes*. Thank you in advance for providing this chance to grow my faith and gain great joy.

In your precious name, *amen.*

Boys to Know Christ

2

Not. a. Thing Looks Like I Thought It Would

A hero is an ordinary individual who finds the strength to persevere and endure in spite of overwhelming obstacles.

—Christopher Reeve

Everything inside me lurched as our used car rattled over the train tracks. I was heading into a gateless neighborhood I was destined to call home for much longer than I wanted to even think about. Surveying the area, I took note that none of the streets had a name. Rows of mobile homes with single-paned windows placed on tiny, rented plots of land lined the unmarked streets. I had been to dozens of neighborhoods just like this one to pick up children for VBS or Sunday school, but today it was different. I was no longer in a luxury vehicle, concerned that neighborhood children would tear up the leather seats. I was not merely pulling up to the curb, patting a child on the back, and dropping him off. Today, I would park in one of the driveways and carry my small child into our new home.

Pain shot through me as I recalled the *No* and the *thing* that had brought me here. God could have intervened, prevented, and stopped the calamity. But He hadn't. Inside I harbored anger, confusion, grief, and loss that seemed to have robbed us blind. Medical bills incurred by our daughter's incident, a stock market crash, and poor choices stripped away everything we knew and held to be dear after 16 years of full-time ministry. A change was urgent and necessary as we were forced to pay for these expenses. I despised the move and the redirection of our career. I was no longer a pastor's wife meeting the needs of others. I was the one with needs. I felt out of place. Reduced. Emptied. At loose ends, with *no* hitting me hard in the gut.

My faith, world, and reality had been shaken, pelted, and all but disintegrated. I loathed this state of *No.thing* and hated the cascade of events that had caused the numbers in my bank account to become nothing—nada! We were starting over at zero.

Feelings of being forsaken, lost, and wondering what on earth God was doing swelled up inside of my chest. The enemy of my soul mocked the years of service we had given to ministry work. He pointed at the beautiful brick houses, parsonage, and church my husband had built with his two hands at no charge for God's cause and whispered that our family would now live in a home resembling a matchbox in comparison.

*One of the hardest things about No.thing is grappling with the reality of no and **wait** by directly applying God's promises to us when life seems to be going in a completely wrong direction.*

It wasn't fair. Not a single thing added up within my theology or inside my head. Where was God?

On this day, as I drove over the tracks and counted the fourth speed bump, God spoke and rattled my very being. "You think you're too good to live here, don't you?" Automatically, "No" fell out of my mouth. But the pain of honesty pierced my heart.

Disgustedly, I shot a glance into my neighbor's messy yard and confessed, "Yes, God, I do!"

The very core of my faith shook. I had lots of questions and wondered, so what's the plan, God, and what just happened to all Your promises to me?

Frankly, it's here that we need help! One of the hardest things about *No.thing* is grappling with the reality of *no* and *wait* by directly applying God's promises to us when life seems to be going in a completely wrong direction. A young man named Joseph didn't have a Bible, but he did have a promise and slugged through this battle the hard way.

Really, I don't deserve this!

Trudging along, staring at the back end of a camel, Joseph must have asked God what was going on as they cruelly carried him away into slavery. We know him as a Bible hero who saved millions of lives during his rule in ancient Egypt (Gen. 45-47). The end of his narrative tells us that God had a plan all along for turning evil into good. But on that day, as his wicked brothers betrayed and sold him, God's promise given to Joseph in a dream became challenged. A no and a wait rudely hit Joseph full on.

As a child, you may have read about the robe of many colors Joseph was given by his father as a sign of belonging and endearment (Gen. 37). Because of this special bond Joseph had with their father, his older half-brothers hated him even more. And the dream?

> "Listen to this dream I had: There we were binding sheaves of grain in the field. Suddenly my sheaf stood up, and your sheaves gathered around it and bowed down to my sheaf."
>
> "Are you really going to reign over us?" his brothers asked him. So they hated him even more because of his dream. (Gen. 37:6-8 CSB)

On a fateful day, revenge took place. The brothers, intending to kill Joseph, stripped him and threw him into a deep empty pit to die. Along came merchants who bound and dragged him into Egypt. There he was sold to Potiphar, an officer of Pharaoh, as his personal attendant. When his master saw that everything he did prospered and that the Lord remained with him, all that Potiphar owned fell under Joseph's authority. Joseph left nothing untouched, except for Potiphar's wife (who continued to throw herself at Joseph day after day). But he refused her advances out of honor for his boss and his God. One day, when everyone was out of the house, she grabbed him (Gen. 39:12). He ran away. Out of spite, she made up the story of attempted rape, and Potiphar had Joseph thrown into prison with no opportunity to defend himself.

What had just happened? A whirlwind of injustice had followed Joseph's dream. In place of servants bowing down to him, he became subjugated to servanthood—not only wrongfully sold into slavery but now falsely accused and punished. Wouldn't you say that he had every right to be hurt, disgusted, and angry? Stripped to nothing, he sat. No family. No job. No help. No future. From all appearances, it seemed that God had failed him. And yet ...

After some time, two of the king's officials were put into custody with Joseph. One night, both men, the chief cupbearer and chief baker, had troubling dreams that made them extremely sad. Since interpretation appeared to be Joseph's specialty, he readily gave them the meaning to both dreams and then asked them for a favor in return.

> And please remember me and do me a favor when all goes well for you. Mention me to Pharaoh, so he might let me out of this place. For I was kidnapped from my homeland, the land of the Hebrews, and now I'm here in prison, but I did *nothing* to deserve it. (Gen. 40:15 NLT, emphasis mine)

I'm writing this fully aware that some of you have had unrealized dreams or ambitions that have turned out unexpectedly or not at all. I want you to see what Joseph saw and get into his head for a minute, because to come out on top, you and I must do exactly what he did—choose in the now to *intentionally* embrace God's promise when it looks *nothing* like our dreams or plans, when the situation we are in is completely out of our control, and it stinks.

Plan A deteriorates to plan B, C, D, and finally F. *No.thing* has a way of turning events to have completely different outcomes than we imagined. Somehow, we think they should go one way, and when they totally go another, we get unhinged. Ultimately, it's up to us to decide what we will do with our feelings, emotions, decisions, and even our thought processes. Yet it's easy to question God, ourselves, or others. It's harder to trust and wait for the goodness of God to show up for us when we need it the most.

Sitting in jail in a foreign country, Joseph could have allowed the no and the wait to sour his spirit and turn him bitter. He didn't. And I'm glad he didn't.

Joseph would be the first to agree that his life had been turned upside down when he found himself as a slave in a foreign land and could no longer rely on daddy or his status as the favorite son. Neither could he count on success from his previous customs or past ways of living. Nothing about this Egyptian lifestyle was normal. Yet Joseph couldn't run away literally, and he refused to shut down intuitively—he didn't quit. He had to examine what was under his feet and then stand on it. He had to deal with what he had now, to become the best person he could be—even when his dreams looked far from his reality.

Consider the following phrases and let this truth bomb set you on fire. Note in verse 15, Joseph says, "For I was *kidnapped* from the land of the Hebrews, and even here I have done *nothing* that they should put me in the dungeon" (emphasis mine).

Joseph uses the word kidnapped. He could have said sold. I'm not sure which would make me feel better—to admit that I was kidnapped by strangers or sold by my brothers. Scripture says kidnapped. So we'll accept that Joseph definitely felt he had been kidnapped.

Notice the narrative a few verses before this in Genesis 39:1 that says it like this, "When Joseph was *taken* to Egypt by the Ishmaelite traders, he was purchased by Potiphar, an Egyptian officer" (NLT, emphasis mine).

Kidnapped. Taken. Terrible plight, horrible life ... until (moment of truth). We read how David later recorded it in Psalm 105,

> Give thanks to the LORD and proclaim his great-
> ness. Let the whole world know what he has
> done.
> Sing to him; yes, sing his praises.
> Tell everyone about his wonderful deeds.
> Exult in his holy name;
> rejoice you who worship the LORD.
> Search for the Lord and for his strength;
> continually seek him.
> Remember the wonders he has performed,
> his miracles, and the rulings he has given ...
> He called for a famine on the land of Canaan,
> cutting off its food supply.
> Then, he *sent* someone to Egypt ahead of them—
> Joseph, who was sold as a slave.
> They bruised his feet with fetters
> and placed his neck in an iron collar.
> Until the time came *to fulfill his dreams,*
> the LORD tested Joseph's character.
> Then Pharaoh sent for him and set him free.
> (v. 1-5, 16-20 NLT, emphasis mine)

Kidnapped? Taken? *Sent!*

Joseph was *not* sold—he was sent!

Awareness is that moment when we realize things didn't go as we planned them, yet providence is right on schedule in our lives. God can leverage our circumstance. The next action is up to us. Will we trust Him with that plan by leaping into His everything?

Digging Deeper

- Where exactly do I believe God is digging deeper inside my character when my personal dream is yet to be fulfilled? *to wait + trust*

- How can my daily words and thoughts reflect that I believe God is working through a no or wait, even if I don't see it? *By not hounding John about his drinking*

- His promise may not include my plan. Am I trusting in His plan or busy trying to create my own? *Let go + Let God*

- I may be in pain, but that doesn't mean I'm not in the center of where God wants me. Do I relate to this? *Is hard to trust when hurting.*

_____

_____

_____

_____

_____

3

Please God ... Do Something!

For the LORD God is our sun and our shield.
  He gives us grace and glory.
*The LORD will withhold **no** good **thing***
  from those who do what is right.

—Psalm 84:11 NLT, emphasis mine

"Watch me, Mommy!" My son happily swung out like a little monkey on the shiny red and blue bars. Hand over hand, he moved spryly to the center of the jungle gym, beaming with pride over his mastery. Within seconds, Markey's hands slipped and he tumbled into the black rubber mulch below. "You're such a big boy," I said as I picked him up and brushed off his denim overalls. He cried out in pain, and I quickly saw that his arm shot out to the side, like a bent arrow.

With an injury so close to the growth plate, an immediate operation for my son was scheduled for the next morning. On our way out of the doctor's office, I stopped by the front desk for last-minute instructions. The receptionist went over the paperwork and informed me that a down payment of $5,000 would be required before the surgery. My throat tightened, and I managed to nod, asking if it were possible to pay early in the morning. I could only hope that something would work out, but I knew we had no funds.

Here I was. Stuck. Again. With *No.thing*.

After our daughter's medical issue and finding our health insurance coverage to be inadequate, we had decided to get smart and change insurance companies. It sounded good at the time, but we soon discovered canceling one before establishing another was a horrible decision. In short, we were classified as "uninsurable" with an existing condition now on her medical record and once again left in a lurch. I needed a miracle.

Crying inside, I hugged my little guy and told him that Jesus would take care of him. If only I knew how. With nothing in our account, no credit cards, insufficient insurance, and no one to ask for help, I had no tangible thing to lean on.

My son's surgery was dependent on a surgeon who required the money down before treating Markey the next morning at 7:00. I prayed, begging God to please help me, or at least have pity on my little boy. If ever I believed in a devil with a pitchfork and tail, it was in that hour of a no and wait, as he hissed steamy insults at my faith, my God, and my *No.thing* that had brought me here.

We didn't have the money and were not eligible for any type of charity. I was left with only one option—to call and cancel his operation.

Despair met me that day.

Unbelief challenged my faith.

"What good has your belief in God been to you?" The enemy spilled his lies. "He's failed not only you but now your son. Do you really want your kids to suffer? What kind of a god would treat you like this anyway?" He continued to berate, "Faith? Oh, you want to be strong for your kids. Why? It's doing nothing for you!"

The very core of my faith, rooted at 12 years old, was shaken. For the first time, I felt betrayed and forgotten by the God who had been my best friend and daddy. The line of demarcation that classified God as a good father who always wanted good for His children had somehow been violated inside my head and left an X across my heart.

My son desperately needed a miracle. I had asked for help, but God was nowhere to be found. Hadn't I taught others that He shows up just when we need it the most? Yet here I had an urgent need and was being let down. I desperately prayed for a yes, and all the evidence pointed to the fact that He had just said no!

My faith was at a breaking point. It had been two full years of severe hardship and setbacks—one after another. Never had I experienced such blackness from the depths of hell. The enemy threatened my soul. He challenged me for not believing God. Everything inside me wanted to have faith.

"Please, God, do something," I prayed and followed with a resolve. "God, I don't know how this is all going to work out— but I *choose* to believe You to make something out of this nothing!"

Choice /Chois/ (*noun*)
1. an act of selecting or making a decision when faced with two or more possibilities." The *choice between* good and evil."

BOOM! That was it. The choice was mine—to fully and confidently believe that God was in charge, that He was good, and that He was fighting *for* my good. Choice couldn't fix my son's arm, but it fixed my gaze upon the One who could.

Do the next thing now.

Daring to believe that He is working even when we don't see it or feel it is the beginning of transforming our now into the next. We then let go and trust someone bigger than a *No.thing*.

I wish I could say I automatically had peace and joy after that moment. But that wouldn't be fair. In hindsight, I can see much more clearly that while my spiritual roots were all in place during that season, I desperately needed them to deepen in a God who was big enough to handle the unexplainable.

During this whole process of learning to trust God entirely, I would repeat over and over in prayer, "God, I believe You love me, that You are in control, and as long as I know You are in this, I will trust You."

Despite circumstantial evidence creating fear and doubt on a human level, I soon discovered that entrusting God with my *now* was the leveraging force that eventually launched me into a world of believing that *No.thing* could actually be a good thing.

If you are sitting in the right now of *No.thing*, you may not be *there* yet, but that's okay. Go ahead and trust Him anyway, for right now.

Go. Up. Now.

We join the story of Elijah during several rough years of drought and famine, and an intense contest between two sides testing whose god was almighty. In the name of the Lord, Elijah triumphed over the priests of Baal, who were on the wrong side of it all, and they were executed. Then we come to the part of the fulfilled promise:

> Then Elijah said to Ahab, "Now, go, eat and drink. A heavy rain is coming." So King Ahab went to eat and drink. At the same time Elijah climbed to the top of Mount Carmel. There he bent down to the ground with his head between his knees.
>
> Then Elijah said to his servant, "Go and look toward the sea."
>
> The servant went and looked. He said, "I see *nothing*."

Elijah told him to go and look again. This happened seven times. The seventh time, the servant said, "I see a small cloud. It's the size of a man's fist. It's coming from the sea."

Elijah told the servant, "Go to Ahab. Tell him to get his chariot ready and to go home now. If he doesn't leave now, the rain will stop him."

After a short time, the sky was covered with dark clouds. The wind began to blow. Then a heavy rain began to fall. Ahab got in his chariot and started back to Jezreel. The Lord gave his power to Elijah. Elijah tightened his clothes around him. Then he ran ahead of King Ahab all the way to Jezreel.
(1 King 18:41-46 ICB, emphasis mine)

Elijah, a mighty prophet of God, saw many miracles performed and come to life. Yet he chose to trust God within the no and the wait. How did he do it? By choosing to believe that God was working in the now, for his next, and for the new thing He would accomplish in the hearts of so many people. While God worked in Elijah's life, He also showed himself strong in the lives of others. We cannot forget this imperative truth that we are an integral part of God's big story. Who knows why God has called you into a time of *No.thing* and how many other people will benefit from the orchestration of God's hand working within that master plan?

> *If I am not content with God's perfect plan in my now, who's to say I will be content with my next or happy with the new?*

We don't have to pretend that everything is sunshine and roses. I don't even have to fake it hoping to make it. But I do need to choose to get up, choose to take the next step, choose to learn in the wait, and choose to grow inside of it, by knowing and believing that God will do the *thing* He has promised He would do.

If I am not content with God's perfect plan in my now, who's to say I will be content with my next or happy with the new? I've got to be okay with myself, with my God, and with my season of now before God will show me the next.

Even after a tremendous victory on Mt. Carmel, the battle still raged. Famine and no rain. Perhaps Elijah's servant needed to see the hand of God working, as his time of waiting included going back to search the sky one more time to see the miracle appear. It took seven times for him, and maybe it's been more for you or someone very close to you. Hold on, friend! God is effectively operating in you, and He is actively working in the lives of others. This *No.thing* will soon become a new thing.

I did call to cancel my son's appointment, explaining that I was not a horrible mother, but we had absolutely no money. A friend called me shortly after, suggesting we go see an orthopedic specialist who might be able to offer some assistance. After an exam and further x-rays, he said he felt confident in trying a series of casts that would heal the bones in time without the need for surgery. We were to meet him the next morning with $500 at the ER, which could not refuse treatment, and he would cast the arm. I hung up the phone, grateful for victory—but the battle still wasn't won. We were still in a drought, with no rainfall on the horizon.

Hoping for a miracle, I checked my banking account and scanned for $500 to miraculously be there. Nothing. Strolling up to the mailbox, I prayed in faith. Nothing. So I went back to scan the sky for rain while tears again poured down my face. Because the battle belongs to the Lord, and *no good thing* will He withhold. Right?

As I tucked my son in, I did the next thing now. I believed that God would somehow show up for him, and we said our bedtime prayers together for the casting that would take place early in the morning.

Awakening later that night, I heard rumbling thunder in the form of a ringing phone. A lady apologetically explained why she was calling so late. She and her husband couldn't go to sleep until they let me know that God had told them to give us $500. She had no idea why. But God did.

Need I tell you to expect heavy rain? Keep looking. Hope may be as small as a fist, but something good is coming next. Get up. Go look. And look again. Do the next thing. Choose to believe. Now!

Digging Deeper

- Why am I ungrateful for the small things God is doing right now in my life by holding out for the big thing?

- In what ways have I put off what I should be doing now?

- When do I freeze up the most relating to or experiencing my faith in God?

- What kind of circumstances or "thing" forces me to my knees, begging for change?

_____

_____

_____

_____

_____

4

And YOU ... Have Done Nothing!

The only limit to our realization of tomorrow will be our doubts of today.

—Franklin Roosevelt

gap (n.)
1. *a break in an object or between two objects*
2. *An unfulfilled space or interval; a break in continuity*

Serving as a ranch hand for a day on the farm is more than I can handle. I quickly discovered this during an interim period, when we moved to a piece of acreage on the outskirts of town. My sister-in-law has a place where we enjoyed the peace and quiet of farm life. Did I just say peace and quiet? Let me explain. There were three horses, three dogs, two cats, 62 chickens, and over a dozen cows roaming a 12-acre plot of land.

Once, when the regular crew was out of town, I became what you call a "desperation" substitute. Although I'm not fond of large animals, I volunteered to do the job for a few days, thinking, *How hard could this be?*

Apparently, it was important to follow the feeding system:

1. Go to the barn and get the horse food. Fill up the alpha male's trough first.

2. Close the gate between horses and cows before feeding the cows.

3. Dump food in cattle feeding troughs.

4. Feed chickens—close their gate on your way out.

5. Make sure the main pasture gate is closed.

6. Change clothes—this is disgusting!

I was a beginner, and day one turned into more than a snafu. It was a total bust. I started with the horses, or should I say, I was 20 minutes late to feed the horses. Regular feeding time began at 5:30 a.m., but anxious about going out into a dark pasture, I waited a few extra minutes, hoping the sun would rise. Bravely, I put on my boots, and after securely fastening the gate behind me, I boldly tramped out through the pasture to do my duty.

With horses following me to the barn, I scooped out the molasses food and made my way to the feeding bins. The bin closest to the barn had fallen on the ground, so I walked past it and on to the far bin, filling bins three and two before going back and placing bin one back on the fence to fill it with feed. Big mistake. I had inadvertently passed the alpha male feeding bin and filled the others first.

Horses get cranky when it comes to their food, and I had just done it all backward. This caused two dominant horses to butt out a third, who followed and began pushing me further inside the barn demanding more chow.

In the meantime, trying to scoop cow feed, I had left the barn door unlatched, which resulted in the entire herd barging in and crowding me into the back of the barn. I panicked! My bravery fled as these wild beasts shoved and snorted. All I could picture was my 130-pound body smashed by these 1600-pound cows. Pinned to the back of the barn and scrambling to get out of there, I found a hole in the barn wall, shinnied through it, climbed around one fence, ran through the chicken coup, and hopped over the other fence.

The cows started to chase me. They picked up speed and were running while I sprinted with buckets flying. A wild stampede behind me, I flung the empty feed buckets to the ground and barely made it through the outside gate. My heart was beating louder than the hooves behind me. My "brave" had started out bold, but it was soon battered.

When I thought all had calmed down, I glanced out and saw chickens scattered throughout the pasture, wildly running in and out of the cows like bugs swarming a porch light. Sixty-two chickens were on the loose! I yelled for my son to rescue me. I couldn't handle all these animals! We rounded up chickens as one dog incessantly barked at a tractor in a nearby field, and the other dog chased the mail truck down the lane.

Dogs barking. Roosters crowing. Cows stampeding. My main thought was *Help! I didn't sign up for this!*

Neither did you. But you find yourself in a place where God calls you into His kingdom. You are committed. You are brave and bold. Things go well, but then somewhere in the middle, an unexplained situation hits you from an unexpected angle. It perplexes and bewilders you. It causes you to feel pinned down and hemmed in. Leaving you battered outwardly and baffled within. Somehow, you get lost in the process and forget the initial promise.

The word *No.thing* resonates with so many of us because we all have experienced a season when we feel nothing, see nothing, or hear nothing. We've experienced that in-between-place of unfilled space, where it's easy to distrust, and the enemy uses the delay to convince us that life is empty and God is to blame.

Moses was at this place, called "in between." The spot between promise and miracle.

Standing out in the wilderness, tending his father-in-law's flock, Moses heard God speak from a burning bush (Exod. 3). This is the same kid whose Israelite mother put him in a basket on the Nile river and was found by an Egyptian princess who raised him as her own. Moses grew up as a prince in Egypt, while his people were slaves. The story really comes alive when this baby discovered his true identity as a Hebrew, and in a fit of rage, killed an Egyptian who was beating one of his kinsmen (Exod. 2).

Forced to flee for his life, Moses lived in the wilderness for close to 40 years until God showed up. He spoke to Moses from the burning bush and told him that his destiny was to return to Egypt. Without a doubt, he had been chosen to lead the children of Israel out of Egypt, but right now, he didn't want that job. He had tried to settle the score years ago when he lived in the palace but ran into a big no and a long wait by taking matters into his own hands and killing a man.

God interrupted the 40-year waiting period and told Moses that he was indeed the man for the job. Eventually, he obeyed and bravely marched into the king's court. We watch the tense exchange:

> Moses and Aaron went to Pharaoh and said, "This is what the Lord, the God of Israel, says: 'Let My people go, so that they may hold a festival to Me in the wilderness.'" Pharaoh retorts, "Who is the Lord? Why should I listen to Him and let Israel go: I don't know the LORD, and I will not let Israel go."
> (Exod. 5:1-3)

Although God had promised Moses that the "I AM" would go before him and lead his descendants into their own land flowing with milk and honey, he still faced opposition and confrontation. Moses had done all the right things by gathering the elders of Israel and telling them that Yahweh had seen their affliction and would rescue them from the Egyptian oppression. It had been a huge pep rally, and within a few short verses, Moses emerged from *beginner* to *brave* and achieved *bold*.

Yet just as he was gaining confidence, he was *baffled* when Pharaoh declared, "Don't reduce the quota. They are lazy. That's why they are crying out, 'Let us go and offer sacrifices to our God.' Load them down with more work. Make them sweat! That will teach them to listen to lies" (Exod. 5:8).

Before the miracle would start, the water could part, and the manna would fall, Moses ran headlong into a *No.thing*. It was taller than a wall of water and bigger than an Egyptian army. In fact, it wasn't the enemy at all who turned on him. It was his own people. The very ones he had come to lead out of captivity.

> The Israelite foreman could see that they were in serious trouble when they were told, "You must not reduce the number of bricks you make each day." As Moses and Aaron left Pharaoh's court, the foreman was waiting outside and said to them, "May the Lord judge and punish you for making us stink before Pharaoh and his official. You have put a sword into their hands, an excuse to kill us!" (Exod. 5:19-21)

Basically, the foreman railed on Moses. "I don't know who you think you are or what ego trip you are on—but you stink at your job! This deliverance thing you are shooting for is off the mark—we are drowning in our own sweat."

TRUST Issues

*Then Moses went back to the LORD and protested,
"Why have you brought all this trouble on your own people, LORD? Why did you send me? Ever since I came to
Pharaoh as your spokesman, he has been even more brutal to your people. And you have done **nothing** to rescue
them!"*

—Exodus 5:22-23 NLT, emphasis mine

The gap widened. Moses felt like God was failing and not living up to His side of the deal. Moses had stepped out of his comfort zone by obeying and declaring the word of the Lord, yet he perceived that God was doing nothing in return. The gaps become visible to us by the words of Moses in these four ways:

1. Moses debunks the compassion of God for His people: "Why have You brought all this trouble on Your own people, LORD?"

2. He disputes the call of God on his life: "Why did You send me?"

3. He discredits the command of God over the situation: "Ever since I came to Pharaoh as Your spokesman, he has been even more brutal to Your people."

4. Finally, he denounces God's care of His people: "And You have done *nothing* to rescue them!"

This is the result of trust issues. When I start thinking I have the right answers and that God is just keeping silent, God appears callous to me, as if He's withholding Himself from my situation. Moses was following a God-inspired "call" on his life, and many people depended on him. Now the reality of fulfilling the mission of that position looked bleak.

Put yourself in the shoes of Moses. Hearing the call of God, knowing what He has asked you to do. Filled with fear and trembling, mustering up the courage to forge through the obstacles and obey God's voice. Make the move. Then to face the giant and speak the words, "Let my people go." It seemed to somehow backfire on him. Moses got the reverse effect when Pharaoh's wrath was poured out and he tasked the people with producing more brick while withholding the straw instead of letting them go.

> No.thing *requires me to separate my feelings from the facts. It's a sticky situation. Calling and appointment must overcome confusion and disappointment.*

No.thing scorned Moses' obedience and laughed in defiance as their resources of straw and stubble were taken away. We wince at his pain and shame. The problem was messy. His words had brought hardship rather than help to the children of Israel, and they were angry. I've been there. When the work I'm trying to accomplish for Christ's kingdom just isn't "working." When nothing glamorous or miraculous happens, and it seems impossible to win. I've found myself, as Moses did, stuck between two groups of angry and angrier people. Have you? With a call to lead people out, but a no thing has trapped you within.

No.thing requires me to separate my feelings from the facts. It's a sticky situation. Calling and appointment must overcome confusion and disappointment. Once I decipher the two, I then have to align myself with God's Word and fully trust it to the end. I have found this one thing to be certain—I cannot allow the thermostat of my feelings to dictate the temperature of my faith. Emotions will not rule me. Situations must not reign. Only trusting the truth will set me completely free.

But Moses hadn't reached that point yet. He was still processing his reality and insecurity.

He had done what God had told him to do. He had been bold. Pharaoh had been told. And now, disappointment over the lack of God's immediate movement to the mission in that moment rested upon Moses' lips: "You have done *nothing* to rescue them."

While I am not covering for Moses, I am relating that our relationship with God has to be open. We need to be real, direct, and honest, and I strongly believe it's okay to vocalize our disappointment to Him. In fact, it is healthy to verbalize rather than internalize our emotions of hurt and distress over situations we don't understand. This is where we verify the calling of God upon our lives and clarify that His promise is still working when our plan is failing. We realize in the middle of our pain, tears, frustration, and confusion that He is the one who has called us from a "burning bush" for a purpose. And if He has brought us out, He will bring us in just like He did for Moses.

Situations have an uncanny ability to shake our settled positions when the conditions of life get out of whack, but God's compassion and calling don't waver. He isn't shaken, and your transformation is still the goal. He cares. Take a second glance and catch sight of the same God who appears to be doing nothing in your life right now. He is the same God who carried you yesterday, is listening to you today, and fighting for you tomorrow.

Go ahead and tell Him your disappointment, but be quick to trust Him now for what He is doing behind the scenes. Your next is right around the corner. He will make all things new, and you will know it soon. I dare you to believe the truth and trust again. Remember the goodness of God in your life. Refuse to allow what seems like a *No.thing* to control your thoughts and responses with negativity.

Digging Deeper

- Was Moses' nothing a delay or a no?
- Even when life gets real, how does God's call remain relevant?
- How has disaster baffled and shaken you up?
- Can you relate to Moses in a time when it seemed God failed you? How was He working behind the scenes?

_____

_____

_____

_____

_____

_____

_____

_____

_____

_____

5

The Divine Fermata!

When you let go and learn to trust God, it releases joy in your life. And when you trust God, you're able to be more patient. Patience is not just about waiting for something ... it's about how you wait, or your attitude while waiting.

—Joyce Meyer

I was humiliated in the fifth grade by a dot and a swat. Grammar just wasn't my thing. In fact, I ended up in the principal's office and received my punishment with a wooden paddle because I had cheated in grammar class. I had creatively found the answers to my assignments, and with a red pen, placed tiny crimson dots to mark where the punctuation should have been. Over simple dots, I learned a hard secondary lesson that day, with a sore behind and a crushed ego.

Since then, I have found that punctuation marks are necessary for readers to catch the finer details in my writing. I have learned the benefits of using punctuation to break up those long sentences. As a writer, I use punctuation to clearly define the message. I don't merely want you to see the printed text. I want you to hear my voice, feel the pathos of my sympathy, and experience my excitement. I want you to know the throb of my heart and to understand the beat of your own while visualizing your personal scenario between the lines. I'm finding out that the dots *do* matter, and the pauses they create enhance dialogue—in fact, enhance everything.

In grammar, every dot has meaning. In the same way, when we accept that a series of dots has meaning, we learn the benefits and the value of the pause.

But in day-to-day life, why do we hate the pause so much? Is it possible that a *no* has proceeded the *wait*, making it appear to be a big black blob while we are still waiting for the *thing* to show up for us?

In writing, we understand that to begin a new paragraph, we must end another. To draft a subsequent chapter, we must close the previous. However, the pause does not lessen the purpose of the proceeding words; rather, it intensifies the significance of what follows. It is a continuation of the story, song, or verse.

> The *no* may have shaken you up. And the *wait* is causing you to doubt, but I want you to realize the *thing* God has for you will begin to unfold.

Often, God does the same in our lives by bringing us to a complete halt. Sometimes the dots of His providence appear to stand out like random marks on a page with no connecting lines. We try to make sense out of them in our lives, but we cannot wrap our brains around them.

No and *wait* seem brutal when we fully expect something to happen, but experiencing a wait does not mean that this is the end of the story. You are in the middle. Waiting is not the *end* for you!

"My thoughts are *nothing* like your thoughts," says the LORD, "And my ways are far beyond anything you could imagine.

For just as the heavens are higher than the earth, so
    my ways are higher than your ways and my
    thoughts higher than your thoughts.
The rain and snow come down from the heavens
    and stay on the ground to water the earth.
They cause the grain to grow,
    producing seed for the farmer
    and bread for the hungry.
It is the same with my word.
    I send it out, and it always produces fruit.
It will accomplish *all* I want it to,
    and it *will prosper* everywhere I send it."
(Isa. 55:8-11 NLT, emphasis mine)

The *no* may have shaken you up. And the *wait* is causing you to doubt, but I want you to realize the *thing* God has for you will begin to unfold. He sees your innermost potential, and He's got your utmost purpose in focus. The word for you is not termination but determination!

What if God is being merciful and bringing you to a full stop before proceeding to the next chapter—the next season—the next "thing" He has for your life? This season of no and the space of wait is giving you time to grow, to learn, and to flourish. It's producing fruit and accomplishing His good pleasure within you.

Don't get tricked into pushing ahead too soon. It's much easier to believe there is good inside of our "next" while missing the value of the now that is working all things good within us. Without a doubt, our next thing is wrapped inside of our now thing. Those layers and processes of wait and space build our character by leveraging or empowering us. In my situation, the paradigm of *No.thing* had to change in my mind before it changed anywhere else. I had to embrace the good within my now to *get* to my next.

See, it all has to do with perception and placement, in that very order, with our perception *of* the placement. Consider this:

In math, a (.) dot by itself is basically meaningless. Dots and zeros by themselves mean absolutely nothing. But when something is added to them, they can mean a whole lot. Imagine a series of zeroes nestled between a couple of (,) commas, with a 1 placed firmly in front of them. Now that, my friend, could amount to something significant indeed, especially, if that combination is then preceded by a ($) dollar sign and lands in your bank account!

Rest assured that when God is added to our nothing, He makes something miraculous in our lives. Nothing is something.

With the above argument of the importance of a strategically placed (.) in math as well as in grammar, I ask again—why does it upset me when a pause shows up in real life? Could it be that it represents an unknown duration of time for which I am not willing to wait?

Maybe you feel like your life is at a period that signifies a pause in your chapter. An end. Has it created suspense, an unfinished thought, or maybe just awkward silence?

I watched a certain vocalist perform for a panel of judges on a season of America's Got Talent. Seconds into the first few stanzas, a brilliant music mogul sitting behind a red buzzer shot his hand in the air. Suddenly, the music stopped and negative energy rushed into the now-silent room. The musician's face showed utter shock and devastating disappointment as the judge blurted, "Wait! I don't like this."

Tears immediately came to my eyes. How could he stop her so abruptly? I loved the song, and it was beautifully sung. It had to be a cruel joke.

The meaning became clear soon enough, as this judge asked the woman if she had another song she could try. Slowly gazing up, she nodded.

Again, the music began. But this time, the most angelic soprano voice flooded the auditorium. Cameras swept the audience, finally landing on the face of the initial judge now beaming and moving his head in affirmation. The vocalist glowed with renewed self-assurance and confidence. She had found her voice after an awkward pause and a melodious tune that truly showcased the deepest beauty of her vocal range. The reason for the "no" and "wait" became crystal clear. The master had heard something much deeper, and in his wisdom, was reaching inside to pull out the fullest talent of this woman.

True, the first song represented weeks of practice and hours of tweaking. Possibly years of dreaming what it would be like to get noticed on the big stage. And in seconds, with the swoop of a hand, it all ended abruptly.

Had her efforts been wasted? Was the *no* cruel? It seemed so to me, and I can only imagine how it felt to her in the moment. Crushing. But when the silence comes, we must trust the One who has called for it. Our divine judge, our loving Father, knows exactly where to put a pause.

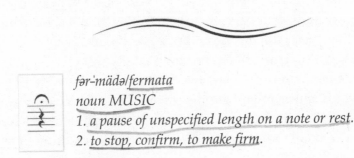

fər-ˈmädə/*fermata*
noun MUSIC
1. *a pause of unspecified length on a note or rest.*
2. *to stop, confirm, to make firm.*

In music, a dot with an eyebrow over it is called a fermata. At its simplest, the fermata (or hold) is a sign that indicates the prolonging of either a sound or a silence. It is drawn as a half-circle with a dot centered along its bottom and is a musical notation placed above a note that should be prolonged beyond the normal duration that its note value would indicate. Exactly how much longer it is held is up to the discretion of the performer or conductor.

I first learned about this notation while taking piano lessons as a kid. A pause didn't mean much to me then, but I learned its value as my musical career grew.

Our community college performed the full three-hour oratorio of George Frideric Handel's Messiah every Christmas. Each year, members of the community were given opportunities to audition for the college chorale. I made the cut and felt privileged to be included for several years with the Augustana Community Choir Christmas performance. The massive rush of emotions as the pipe organ, harpsichord, violins, and instrumental movements played was indescribable.

Our well-established conductor could be a stickler and knew rhythm was key to this original masterpiece. Rehearsals were intense, and he demanded nothing less than perfection. Never will I forget one practice, midway through singing with over 500 voices, when our conductor abruptly shut down the entire thing. The room fell eerily silent as he stared us down. Then he pointed his baton directly at a college student sitting in the third row, who had been tapping his toe to the beat of the music.

"Never do that again! I'm the conductor."

While our conductor remained in full control of every individual voice and every single instrument, we had to keep our eyes on him. The timing was controlled by the man with the baton. At any point, he could hold a note for two or three more beats if he chose. The fermata became the tipping point of emotion, specifically designed for dramatic effect. For the crescendo to build, we had to learn to play the pause. Merit was found in the wait.

Don't be afraid of the *no* and the *wait*. It never feels good in the middle, but God is pulling something fuller and richer out of you. He's pouring His grace deeper into that empty space. You may not see it now but keep trying and trusting.

After that day in Mr. Principal's office, my grammar teacher endeared herself to me. You know why? She had determined to use my *bad* to become my greatest *good*. From that day forward, she spent hours working with me on diagramming, writing, grammatical errors, and yes ... punctuation. It paid off! I'm now writing with confidence and using all those pauses, allowing God to fill in those empty spaces with His words.

I encourage you to get your head up and stop feeling like everything is for nothing. Quit tapping your toe and follow God's beat. I believe your no and wait might be the key to unlocking the treasure of your heart. Go ahead and speak to that tension you are sensing. It could be the beginning of what God is going to use to propel you from your *No.thing* into your next thing.

The music of your life may have paused. But the wait will make you great!

Digging Deeper

- Where in my life do I best find no and wait to be growing me?

- Have I continued to stretch myself during a season of wait?

- How can I still sing despite what seems like a setback?

- Do I have a story I can tell of God's faithfulness within a period of no or wait?

Pat - John passed away a year ago
Funel mercies for Eleen
Parker - broke up = girlfriend

Section Two

Next thing

Proc·ess (n.)/ ˈprä ̧ses, ˈprōses/
1. a series of actions or steps taken in order to achieve a
   particular end.

6

The Shift

(When Nothing Else Gives)

It's what you do next that counts.

—Jamie Reagan from Blue Bloods[1]

I've been known to shift conversation between friends at the dinner table or coffee bar. I've even attempted to create more spontaneity in others by playing devil's advocate and shifting unengaging dialogue during a church board meeting where, yes, everyone had previously been bored.

Maybe you have been guilty of doing the same—shifting a compliment someone gives you on a new outfit by deflecting with "Oh, I've had this for a while." Why not accept it with an honest smile and thank you? Or how about when someone tells you the speech, event, or small group you led was amazing? Why not accept the praise with grace?

We've all at one time or another been guilty of slightly shifting or moving a conversation, compliment, or even possibly blame from one place to another. This kind of shifting is not always helpful.

But there's a *good* kind of shifting I want to discuss—and that involves our thought process. I strongly believe that culture yells at us, and our own selves tell us this lie: that *No.thing* is a problem, an issue. For example, if you are found with *No.thing*—fill in the blank [no kids, no home, no fame, no recognition, no career, no name, etc.] it is definitely portrayed as a negative thing. Yet there are truths in the Bible clearly showing us that *no thing* could be a *positive thing*. We just need to shift our thinking.

I grew up relatively poor, with a single mother who struggled to meet our basic needs. I didn't have the problem like a lot of my friends, who sorted through a pile of shoes at the bottom of their closet to find a match. Every year, when it came time to shop for school supplies and shoes, my sister and I had one opportunity to make the most of our money. I was selective in my choice of school shoes because one dress pair and one gym pair had to last me all year long. We penny-pinched, scrimped, and got by. It wasn't easy, but it shaped who I became as a young woman and adult.

With that said, you can understand why more always means less to me. Since I don't like clutter and am not sentimental, I've been known to weed out and live pretty minimalistically. My basic mantra is, *bring one thing in, and two things go out*. (Let's not talk about the time I threw away all the tax papers. My hubby nearly lost his entire mind—so I won't go there.)

But it's true—too much stuff clogs up my system and stifles my spirit. Just ask my kids, and they will tell you that I love to organize and purge. "Give me three large trash bags and I can clean this entire room in nothing flat ... You do it or I will. Trust me. It will all be gone."

Cleaning is a calming thing. Organizing is great. So you can imagine my perfect delight when a friend called and asked if I could help her get "a few things in order" before her new baby arrived. I accepted with pure glee with thoughts of arranging a cute little baby room.

The next day I walked in, ready to move, plow, shift, and change things. I was up for the challenge. Totally. Give me two hours, and I will lick up this entire baby room.

I just didn't know that my paradigm was going to be hit with the biggest shift ever, as my friend showed me not only one but *three* rooms that we were going to basically flip upside-down and completely turn around.

By this, I mean "rearrange" and totally change. Beds. Dressers. Closets. Bookcase ... *everything*.

I hadn't geared up for this but decided to be brave. "Boxes," I said out loud, "We need boxes to sort things: save, sell, throw."

I left for her garage to search for any kind of containers or storage totes and then dragged my cargo back upstairs to find my very pregnant friend bending and pitching toys, blankets, stuffed animals, shoes, dress-up clothes, and books into a mammoth-sized pile.

My heart beat a little faster; this is not what I had pictured. So much for sorting—that would come later.

Here's the deal: sometimes creating space looks like one giant pile-up! We get so disappointed when it isn't pretty—nothing how we imagined it. Making space might look like one word: upheaval!

It's not Pinterest-y or Joanna Gaines worthy, and it sure doesn't look wholly or holy, however you slice it.

On that morning, with hair flying and sweat pouring, my friend knew that we needed room to work, and she was massively creating it!

See, the problem with our thinking is the same issue I had with arranging the baby room. I wanted to sort through all the things to categorize, label, and dump. My friend had a bigger picture in mind. She just needed space!

Honestly, if we ever intend to make space for change, we will have to shift our current method of thinking. First, I want you to analyze your *No.thing* and expect possibilities for a good thing. God did. Every evening during the six days of creation, He called His work good. When He started, nothing but void could be found. "He stretches out the north over empty space; He hangs the earth on *nothing*" (Job 26:8 NKJV). God had a clean canvas with no *thing* there to get in the way. Don't be alarmed when you get nothing but white space. Flip that thought by embracing the space as something that is making room for your next.

Did you know that in page layout, white space is frequently referred to as *negative space* because it is the unprinted area, margin, or border that is left unmarked? However, many companies are using white space to their advantage. They are finding that less is more, realizing that a crowded, busy, illustrated page over-stimulates the eye and doesn't allow the reader the opportunity to breathe or take in important information. It's like finding Waldo. Businesses consider negative space as a positive means to innovatively fill a niche of opportunity that could be otherwise lost on a busy page. Less is more.

It reminds me of the life many of us live. In a global society crammed full of digital media distractions, our inputs are higher than ever before. We become overwhelmed with the mass expanse of humanity and problems that never were ours to fix in the first place. Modernized economics and commercialism drive us to get and buy more, while our closets are bulging, garages and attics are overflowing. If that isn't enough, we can always rent a storage shed down the road so we can hoard and store more stuff. Raise a hand if this sounds familiar.

Too much of a good thing is too much! Up-leveled living requires some things to disappear. Clutter in our homes and living areas causes brain drain. We trip over senseless amounts of things. Outgrown clothing, out-of-date items, and out-of-place things are outputting our good use of energy. It's time for these zapping "extras" that steal our productivity to find another home. Shift them all into a box and donate to your local charity. Get rid of them. You could use a blank slate.

Before the shutdown of 2020, "Crazy busy" had become the norm, running from soccer to basketball and catching fast food in between. Rushing from one meeting to another. Putting out fires. Scheduling events back to back, while trying to juggle it

> *The season of No.thing is here to create space for grace.*

all. With jumbled thoughts and days, we fill our lives and heads so full that we've given ourselves no space to grow, to breathe, or to live.

In fact, we have become an entitled group of people living in a free nation where many feel we have a right to full refrigerators, full cupboards, and full stomachs. *No.thing* blows our entire mindset. We expect fullness—a full schedule, spreadsheet, and social calendar; full churches, full pews, and full groups. We book full-time college classes and work overtime hours. Full, we must be full!

But what if God needs a space that is large enough, uncluttered enough, and empty enough to receive a fullness that cannot be matched by anything else we can conjure up? What if God wants to fill us up with Himself—is there room? Room in your mind, room in your heart, room in your house, room in your schedule—is there room?

The season of *No.thing* is here to create space for grace. Space to rest. Space to re-position, re-group, and re-think. Space to trust and space to heal.

I challenge you to step into your now and make the shift, my friend, by prayerfully asking yourself and God: How can I better use this space You have given to me?

Digging Deeper

- In what way do I sense God leading me to make space?

- What upheaval causes me to question or trust God's providence?

- How can I better use the space God has given to me?

- Who will benefit from me making this shift?

_____

_____

_____

_____

_____

_____

_____

_____

_____

7

Reframe and Rename

Faith is taking the first step even when you don't see the whole staircase.

—Martin Luther King Jr.

An ad for MLK hipster eyeglass wear recently caught my attention, describing them as, "A statement in simple, unmitigated, and timeless elegance. Like the man, be great."

It made me curious, as I don't ever recall seeing any pictures of Martin Luther King Jr. wearing glasses in any of my school textbooks or in documentaries. Since he died at the young age of 39, I proceeded to dig deeper into whether he was possibly nearsighted or needed glasses only for readers.

As I sifted through resources searching for pictures and articles, I came across this interesting tidbit. An exhibit honoring Martin Luther King in the Atlanta airport displays a pair of eyeglasses he sometimes wore. The sign below the case states the following:

> Although he didn't need them, Martin Luther King Jr., thought glasses made him look distinguished.[1]

Perception, or what others thought of him, seemed to be important to Martin Luther King. Yet his perspective or viewpoint of himself and of his people was, by far, more reaching.

Heroic civil rights leader Martin Luther King came from nothing as a child, yet undoubtedly his tenacity and vision changed the world. He was a forward-reaching person who had a dream for culture and society, one who could imagine change. Transcending the "thing" life had thrown at his entire race, Martin Luther King refused to allow his *No.thing* to restrict his *next thing*. That would eventually give birth to an era of *new things* for his people. But how?

He chose to reframe the hurt into a message of hope for all races and genders across cultural and political boundaries. King's sense of value and success came from within him before anything happened outside of him.

I don't want to admit I have a problem, but clearly, I do. Having perfect eyesight until recently, I've never worn glasses and was really comfortable with the convenience of my naked eye. But recently, I noticed that I am squinting to read menus and reading text messages is becoming an issue. The trouble? My perspective is off, my vision blurred. I've put it off for over a year, trying to cope, but the truth is I need readers. I obviously can't see clearly.

Finding New Begins with Your Next

We don't have to pretend nothing is wrong. But I do have to choose to get up, choose to take the next step, and choose to learn in the wait and grow inside of it by reframing how I think. I need to know and believe that God will do the *thing* He has promised He would do. If I am not content with my now, who's to say I will be content with my next or happy with my new? I've got to take a realistic look at my situation right now while continuing to fully believe God for both the next and the new.

We must implement this mindset now if we want our next to be different. Mind-brain-reality is summed up in this quote from cognitive neuroscientist Dr. Caroline Leaf: "I control my next reality in this very moment by actually possessing the power to change my brain by the way that I think now. It affects the pattern of my future thinking."[2] It's true. Our next is actually beginning now. The hurt of today can become a tool of hope for tomorrow.

I frequently listen to *Cleaning Up the Mental Mess,* Leaf's practical podcast that has been extremely helpful to me in challenging my thinking. Specializing in neuropsychology over 30 years of clinical studies and author of several books, including *Switch On Your Brain,* Dr. Leaf teaches that our minds essentially drive our next reality. Her studies prove that our current thought pattern literally becomes or grows the new cells of our brain and establishes the foundation of what we will say and do next. I love this quote from one of her podcasts and repeat it often: "You can change anything in your life by how you manage that situation in your mind. Although we cannot many times change our political, societal, or economical station or situation, we can control the way we view them."

We tend to get this skewed in our minds because our culture and society define success by our reality, yet we've got to be at peace within ourselves, with our God, and with our now, which is literally preparing our next. Living based upon others' perception of me is exhausting and non-effective. What really counts is our perspective of God and the work *He* can do inside of us. This is the leveraging key.

Bottom line, our peace and success are settled within, not from an outside source. Therefore, it merits asking, *How am I viewing my No.thing reality, and what kind of next thing am I actively creating?*

Per cep tion (n)
1. The ability to see, hear, or become aware of something through the senses.
2. A way of regarding, understanding, or interpreting something; a mental impression

I'm not asking you to be fake or someone you are not. Yet perception is one of the core elements of our thinking process. It's where we decide what we will carry out. Perception is not necessarily reality, but it shapes how we perceive our reality. Maybe your perception of life began as a survival mechanism to shield you from childhood wounds, and it continued into adulthood with each pain of disappointment. Or maybe you're a little like me, holding tightly to what seems safe, even if it is a nothing.

Often, *No.thing* is a negative attitude—a frame of mind. It's not necessarily a situation, condition, circumstance, or a time in space but my perception of that space. It's not a "shapeshift" but a *life shift* decision of finding and living the full life God has for us in every moment of every season, whether it's good or bad. I wasn't able to fully grasp the benefits of reframe and rename, until the paradigm of my thinking shifted.

Re-frame (verb)
1. Place in a new frame
2. Frame or express (words, concept, or plan) differently

The word "reframing" naturally hit me as something or someone trying to portray an image in a different light—a filter of sorts, viewing only the pretty, positive, petite angles. Social media has mastered the art of revealing the perfect picture of wealth, health, happy, and #blessed.

I pushed back on this concept of reframing and renaming for a long time because I didn't want to be pretentious and for sure wouldn't be caught believing the fictitious. (Just like not wanting to wear the readers). After all, I could see "fine." But could I?

Reframing is activating in a positive manner what I know to be true about the *thing* God has in store for me and shifting my mindset to reframe the *No.thing* by doing that very next thing, which will set the course for the new thing God has planned for me.

This pivotal shift came to me when I realized that I was not merely rationalizing or pretending the *No.thing* away. On the contrary, while my situation and position remained the same, I chose to reframe my thinking on that circumstance as a place in time, one in which God had chosen for me to draw closer to Him.

Reframe is more than merely putting a different twist on the same picture. It's not being fake. Fake is a sham, when something isn't original, genuine, or real. Your issue is real, but reframing softens the insecurity we feel when facing the uncertainty of our *No.thing*. Reframing puts the controls in God's hands and affirms our unwavering faith in a powerful God.

> *If your No.thing has immobilized you, begin with the small step of reframing that situation from hurtful to hopeful.*

Doing the *next thing*, whatever that may be for you, requires that kind of faith. Believing God is ordering our steps and causing something good within them. "The Lord directs the steps of the godly. He delights in every detail of their lives" (Ps. 37:23 NLT). All of us want a simple five-step plan to victory, but many times the framework around that picture is much more complicated than that. I've talked to women about their hurts on matters of weight, divorce, infertility, mental health issues, and even cancer. These ladies all had one thing in common—they reframed their hurt into hope by taking life one day at a time, one step at a time. And while those steps were extremely difficult, they realized the value of reframing by doing the next thing directly in front of them.

If your *No.thing* has immobilized you, begin with the small step of reframing that situation from hurtful to hopeful. Take one simple step. It may seem minuscule. You will be surprised to find that small steps today bring you more fully into your next thing. Always keep in mind the potential of movement.

Amy Grant said it this way, "If it all just happened overnight, you would never learn to believe in what you cannot see."[3] Seeing is believing and then acting upon that belief.

Moving up the Mountain

If you have ever tried to marathon, hike, or mountain climb, you realize that pacing yourself is key. Steady wins the race. As we consistently reframe our hurt into a message of hope, it not only builds endurance but systematically takes us to the next level. You *will* reach the top. The view is breathtaking, and all the pain you endured getting there will be worth it. You might be wondering if it's too late for you.

At the mature age of 70, the father of faith was promised the entire land of Canaan. Yet when God called Abram to move from his hometown of Ur of the Chaldees, "he went out even though he did not know where he was going" (Heb. 11:8 NIV). All Abraham knew was that he was supposed to step out before God would bring him in. The move to the unknown transported Abram across the country to fulfill his end dream—a child!

In the original Hebrew language, the name Abram means *exalted father*, yet in his old age, there was still no child. In conjunction with his covenant, God renames him Abraham, which literally translates as *father of a multitude,* and from his lineage, the entire Jewish race was born. This is significant to note—the father of faith wasn't always a father, both literally and theoretically. He got there by taking character-building steps of faith when he had nothing but this promise—that a son as his inheritance would multiply to become more than the stars in the night sky, while he and his wife Sarah remained infertile for 30 long years.

To top it all off, when this promised child finally arrived and was living under Abraham's roof, God asked this father to take his beloved son to Mount Moriah and sacrifice him as a burnt offering. I'm guessing Abraham didn't sleep a wink that night, and bets are he didn't share the full story with Sarah either. Alone, he struggled all night.

The very next morning, Abraham got up early, loaded his donkey, and set out for the place God had told him about. On the third day of their journey, Abraham stopped and told the servants to wait for him and Isaac to return. He then placed the wood upon Isaac's shoulders while he himself carried the fire and the knife. Continuing up the mountain, Isaac turned and asked, "Father? We have the fire and the wood, but where is the sheep for the burnt offering? 'God will provide a sheep for the burnt offering, my son,' Abraham answered" (Gen. 22:8 NLT).

This story of a dad taking the next step in obedience is deeply significant and deserves our consideration. When Abraham lifted the knife to kill his son, an angel commanded him to stop, and then he saw a lamb caught in a thicket. A sacrifice was provided, and with the lamb in place of his son, Abraham worshiped the Lord and renamed the place *"the Lord will provide"* (Gen. 22:14). Hence, by reframing and renaming, Abraham's life was built upon the complete belief in a *"God who brings the dead back to life and who creates new things out of **nothing**"* (Rom. 4:17 NLV, emphasis mine).

I can't even imagine the contortions Abraham's heart and mind had to go through, yet he didn't try to skip from *no thing* to *new thing* without completing the *next thing*. For Abraham, it was a step-by-step process. He had to get up, load the donkey, take his son, leave the house, climb the mountain, and then lay his son upon the altar before the lamb appeared. He built faith. Reframing and renaming worked for him. The new thing did come, but the whole time his mindset was one of obedience as Abraham took one step at a time. Whatever circumstance your *No.thing* throws at you, I challenge you to reframe and rename it, just like the father of faith did.

I'll go ahead and break the news—if you're still looking for the "next" and "new" to magically appear for you without putting in the work of changing your mindset, then it's high time for you to obey and do that next thing. Now!

Reframe and Rename

- Stop calling that kid your problem child and rename him your possibility kid.

- Instead of saying, "I bombed it," reframe and say, "I'm working on it."

- See yourself through God's lenses rather than comparing yourself to others.

Give your issue a new name by looking at what it can be with God's help.

I ask again, are you seeing clearly? Maybe it's time we put the glasses on and see our hurt, pain, and no thing differently than ever before. Don't overlook the lessons learned and wisdom gained from them. You have something important to say and something valuable to contribute to society. It's time we see the next thing that progressively leads us from our no thing and inspires us to actively step into a new thing.

Even if we don't think we need glasses. Let's put them on!

Digging Deeper

- What excuse do I keep using to justify where I am in my spiritual journey?

- Is my attitude preventing me from taking the next step of faith?

- How can I reframe my hurt into a message of hope?

- What steps of faith can I take to reach the higher place God is asking me to go?

_____

_____

_____

_____

_____

_____

_____

8

Pull Out the Cotton Balls

Since God knows our future, our personalities, and our capacity to listen, He isn't ever going to say more to us than we can deal with at the moment.

—Charles Stanley

Ever wondered why you cannot get that song or jingle out of your head that seems to be playing on repeat? The power of the ear or "earpower" is an amazing gift to humanity. Some would argue that hearing is the most important sense.

Neuroscientist Seth Horowitz describes how hearing shapes the mind and, most uniquely, how sounds communicate to the brain far more quickly than sights. While light travels faster than sound, its pathway to the conscious brain is slower. Supporting this, Dr. Horowitz states, "Vision maxes out at 15 to 25 events per second, while hearing is based on events that occur thousands of times per second."[1]

The science of sound is fascinating—how we hear and what we hear, and most importantly, how we *interpret* what we hear.

Misheard lyrics are so hysterical. Like this well-known Christmas song and its variation, "Olive, the other reindeer, used to laugh and call him names…" or "Joy to the world, the Lord has gum." There's a funny name for this phenomenon: mondegreen. It's a word defined as mishearing or misinterpretation of a phrase in a way that gives it new meaning. To be honest, this explains a lot. Clearly, we've all (at one time or another) had communication issues to work out.

For example, my sister and mother got into a verbal tangle when I was in high school. It all began with a simple question. My mom was washing dishes at the sink, and my sister was sitting at the table doing her homework. "Hey, Mom, were you in the Civil War? I mean, did you have anyone in your family fighting in the Civil War?"

Mom laughing: "Well, yes, everyone had silverware back in my day."

Sister: "Did you know that the Polish used a knife-gun combo called a flintlock ax to fight in their Civil War?"

Mom: "Absolutely, you can polish knives if they are real silver, but why would anyone leave gum on their knife?"

Sister: "No, Mom, you've got it all wrong!"

We still laugh over that conversation. It was a simple, and might I add harmless, mishearing. Mom had her hands in soapy warm water and silverware on her mind. Sister had her eyes on a history textbook.

Miscommunication occurs in big ways and small ways; some instances create laughter, but most cause frustration and even anger. We can miss out on rewarding benefits. Upgrading our *No.thing* to God's yes requires a collaboration of our senses, meaning we not only have to change our mindset and refocus our eyesight but additionally, we have to hone in on our hearing.

Undoubtedly, words can get tangled and new meanings applied to those words. Sound has a remarkable impact on the workings of our brains, and fine-tuning our brains plays a large part in how we process what we hear. Are we paying attention to what we hear and how we hear?

Our next best thing may very well be listening intently for God's voice—not what we want to hear but truly hearing what we need to hear to make the best choice for our next step. What is God saying?

Hearing includes asking questions—lots of them. Hearing includes seeking solutions. Hearing involves listening with devotion.

Ineffective listening creates misunderstandings, missed opportunities, and mistrust. Conflict and overall defeat could be avoided by taking the time to listen rather than jumping at the first conclusion and making a hurried decision.

I could have been spared if I had listened longer and a little bit harder.

Earlier, I mentioned that medical issues and underinsurance spiraled our family into a financial crisis, but the beginning of that story is this: Success in the stock market had provided us with a handsome sum. With a sufficient cushion and nest egg, we decided to buy a piece of property to someday build a house for retirement. Our car and truck were paid for, but they were older and not nearly as shiny as the ones we wanted. We heard people say that leasing vehicles was the only way to go. Sounded good! So we leased two pricey cars at $650 each and traded our $0 a month car payment for $1,300. Additional purchases like new furniture made sense to us—we needed it, right?

But when the stock market crashed, the medical bills mounted, and all the things piled up, we were in over our heads. There is no way we could see what was around the corner. I'm not crying over spilled milk, but I do realize that had we taken a little more time to pray and invested a bit more effort into listening, we could have made better choices.

A Costly Mistake

Worth millions of dollars, she appeared foolish in the heart of New York City on New Year's Eve. A celebrity stood with mic in hand, trying to get her cue. She didn't recover and was ridiculed by thousands for a less than par performance—an embarrassment to herself and her fans. What happened?

It's now four minutes to showtime. She says, "I hear nothing in my ears; my ears are dead." The other stage manager says, "It will work right when we go live." Then things start to get chaotic. They start counting her down—four minutes, three minutes. Singer: "I can't hear." Them: "You're gonna hear when it goes live—two minutes!"[2]

Then, she goes live but can't hear anything because her earpiece is dead. The artist quickly pulls them out of her ear, hoping to hear the music, but the noise of Times Square and the noise reverberating off the skyscrapers is deafening and chaotic. Without hearing her music, the timing and choreography were a disaster, and all hopes of recovery were lost.

As a woman who follows Christ, this one phrase stood out to me: *"I hear **nothing** in my ears; my inner ears are dead."* I remembered the verse I had read that morning: "My sheep hear my voice, and I know them, and they follow me" (John 10:27KJV).

I'm not exactly sure what happened to this pop singer, but I don't live her life—I'm responsible for me, for my hearing. As children of God, are we hearing His voice on the big stage of life? Is the choreography of our life by His design? Who we listen to matters. I don't ever want to get to the place of distraction, where the voice of the crowd drowns out His voice. What is in your ear, so to speak?

I called across the yard at my hubby, who was happily burning leaves and didn't hear a word I was saying. His voice ramped up in competition to the music blaring through his noise-canceling headphones the kids had given him for Christmas.

I walked further out into the backyard and hollered again. Nothing. A few steps forward and waving this time, while yelling. Still nothing. Frustrated, I tried to find a stick or pinecone to throw in his direction. It was hot outside. All I wanted was to ask if he needed a drink, and he was completely ignoring me.

Kate Murphy says in her book, *You're Not Listening~What You're Missing and Why It Matters,*

> Despite living in a world where technology allows constant digital communication and opportunities to connect, it seems no one is really listening or even knows how. And it's making us lonelier, more isolated, and less tolerant than ever before. Listening is something you either do or don't do every single day. We often deprive ourselves by not listening.[3]

No.thing puts us in this aligned position of searching for the truth, waiting for the right move, and listening for the next word.

Hearing may mean waiting or could mean moving.

Hearing is mental and emotional; to hear takes a clear head and an undistracted heart.

Hearing is both physical and spiritual, allowing us to hear with a rested body and renewed spirit.

> *No.thing has a way of taking the ear plugs out of our ears. It gets our attention.*

Hearing can involve simple, yet practical, self-care on our part, such as resting, eating, and drinking enough water so our bodies can receive a clear message.

Elijah, the prophet who did incredible things for God's cause back in Old Testament days, is a perfect case. Not every day was a victory—he had some discouraging days too. On one of these days, we find Elijah totally exhausted emotionally and lying under a broom tree, voicing to God that he was a failure, finished, and done! He asked that his life would end quickly before falling into a deep sleep. While he was sleeping, a heavenly messenger touched him and said, "Get up and eat" (1 Kings 19:5). Elijah turned and found a breadcake sitting over charcoal near his head. There was also a jar of water. He ate the food and drank the water, and then he lay back down. This happened twice. He slept, ate, and drank.

Then the messenger told him that he would need the added strength for the coming days, which included a 40-day journey to Mt. Horeb, the Mountain of God. Elijah had won some major battles and passionately torn down idols and a bunch of other things, but now he felt like he was the only one left holding down the fort. He was weary and desperately needed to hear from God. Mid-stream, we break in on their conversation.

> Eternal One: "Why are you here, Elijah? What is it that you desire?"
>
> Elijah: "As you know, all my passion has been devoted to the Eternal One, the God of heavenly armies. The Israelites have abandoned Your covenant with them, they have torn down every single one of Your altars, and they have executed by the sword all those who prophesy in Your name. I am the last remaining prophet, and they now seek to execute me as well."
>
> Eternal One: "Leave this cave, and go stand on the mountainside in My presence."
>
> The Eternal passed by him. The mighty wind separated the mountains and crumbled every stone before the Eternal. This was not a divine wind, for the Eternal was not within this wind. After the wind passed through, an earthquake shook the earth. This was not a divine quake, for the Eternal was not within this earthquake. After the earthquake was over, there was a fire. This was not a divine fire, for the Eternal was not within this fire. After the fire died out, there was *nothing* but the sound of a calm

breeze. And through this breeze a gentle, quiet voice entered into Elijah's ears. (1 Kings 19:9-13 VOICE)

Elijah had extremely demanding and high-level assignments. Bulldozing ahead and messing up wasn't an option. Too often, we run forward and are caught up in the motion of *doing* when it's time to be *hearing*. Not so here with Elijah. He was at a place where taking care of his body and listening to the quiet voice gave him not only the next steps for his future but also the directive for anointing his replacement as the future prophet of Israel.

> *We need to find God, and he cannot be found in noise and restlessness. God is the friend of silence. See how nature — trees, flowers, grass- grows in silence; see the stars, the moon and the sun, how they move in silence ... We need silence to be able to touch souls.* —Mother Teresa

The force of culture and the world is battling to distort our hearing. We can also be tainted by what we *want* to hear or altered by what we have previously heard. A calm breeze isn't always the thing we are searching for but is the thing our souls are inherently longing for. Your next thing may clearly be to pull out the earplugs of distraction.

No.thing is leading you to a place that is uncrowded. It's asking you to be a better version of who God made you to be. Consider taking a break from social media, news, and outside commotion. Sweep out the "not good enough" from your inner ear and heart. Create a place to hear God's voice and listen for His next in your life.

> And your ears shall hear a word behind you, saying, "This is the way, walk in it," when you turn to the right or when you turn to the left." (Isa. 30:21 ESV)

God is calling us to walk with Him (and it's possible); are we listening?

Digging Deeper

- Take a moment to ask, why am I here, and what do I most desire?

- How can you leave your cave to go stand in His presence?

- Make a plan. Next, just listen.

_____

_____

_____

_____

_____

_____

_____

9

Set Down Your Water Pot

Doing the best at this moment puts you in the best place for the next moment.

—Oprah Winfrey

Jacqueline is one of those peppy ladies who inspires me to one day "grow up" to be just like her. It seems nothing gets her down, and taking no for an answer isn't even a consideration. So it shocked me to hear her emphatically declare, "When God says no, it really is the best plan." At 23 years old, clutching a brand-new college degree, she was accepted into the Peace Corps and headed for a great adventure in the world. Upon submitting her physical, she packed, planned, and dreamed about her soon departure for Africa's Sierra Leone. Without warning, a *no* hit her in the face after a routine physical exam, revealing ovarian cancer and deeming her unfit for the mission.

> I was devastated and quite angry with God. In fact, I did not speak to Him for many months. While working as a government auditor in sheer boredom, I had plenty of time to reflect on the facts as I saw them—

that my life was over. My only chance for adventure and happiness was gone; it was unfair and mean of God for my life to simply ooze by.

Greater plans were in store for Jacque. Miraculously, she was healed, and soon after, she was flying all over the world delivering United Nations Humanitarian Aid by land and air. Over the span of 26 years, she worked with NASA astronauts, visited both north and south poles, operated satellites in space, served as a university professor, launched nuclear missiles, flew airplanes, glacier hiked in Norway, and lived in a remote part of Italy for two years working with 200 coworkers from 12 different countries. Those discoveries occurred because she accepted her reality and trusted her life to God.

Now, on the threshold of retirement, she is telling her life story and continuing her adventures as a global volunteer and missionary to refugees in Greece.

If I could reach back in time and offer advice to my younger self, I would remind her that we serve a Good Father who is always right and faithful. A Father who has given me more than I could ask or imagine from the nothingness of my immaturity and rebellion. I have learned to love God's response of "No" because it means He has good plans for me, which I cannot even fathom. He has proven it over and over again in my life.

Jacque isn't the only one with control issues. Relinquishing our ideas, plans, and ambitions is one of the hardest things to do. Giving up our way for God's will is often difficult in the moment, but so rewarding in the end. The upgrade He makes in our life far exceeds anything we could have imagined or accomplished on our own.

The woman Jesus met at the well knew she wasn't living a completely righteous life, but she was not easily convinced that a change was necessary. What could this man sitting at the well tell her about religion and relationship that she didn't already know? And why was he, a Jewish man, asking her, a Samaritan woman, for a drink of water?

The water pot at her feet was hers; she had hustled, worked hard, and earned everything in her possession. Some speculated that she had control issues, but they weren't walking in her shoes. With a less-than-stellar reputation, she knew better than most what it meant to live with nothing, running from what was her now thing and searching, searching, searching for the next.

She hadn't always been a total control freak; she had once been open, generous, doing her best to maintain a good life. But broken promises, bashed relationships, and brackish religion riddled with fear had reshaped her—no more trusting anything or anyone but herself.

Then unexpectedly, during her daily trek for water, in the stifling heat of the day, Jesus showed up. He called her out personally and promised to give her something she didn't already have, didn't already know, and hadn't already seen:

> It was about noon. When a Samaritan woman came to draw water, Jesus said to her, "Will you give me a drink?" The Samaritan woman said to him, "You are a Jew and I am a Samaritan woman. How can you ask me for a drink?" (For Jews do not associate with Samaritans) Jesus answered her, "If you knew the gift of God and who it is that asks you for a drink, you would have asked him and he would have given you living water." (John 4:6-10 NIV)

She felt both exposed and threatened, her hackles automatically went up, and she threw a question right back. What do you know, sitting there offering me everything, and I see nothing?

The woman said, "Sir, you have *nothing* to draw with and the well is deep. Where can you get this living water? Are you greater than our father Jacob, who gave us the well and drank from it himself, as did also his sons and his livestock?" (John 4:11 Emphasis mine)

Several previous relationships had brought her to this point, where she was offered fulfillment in exchange for fulfilling others' desires. But this man obviously had *nothing* in his hands to give. He was offering her a drink of water while at the same time asking for a drink of water. What kind of scheme was this anyway?

Jesus answered, "Everyone who drinks this water will be thirsty again, but whoever drinks the water I give them will never thirst. Indeed, the water I give them will become in them a spring of water welling up to eternal life." (John 4:13-14 NIV)

I can see her foot jaunt out from under her dusty robe and a hand settle on her belted hip. You want to run around this topic, do you? Let's go! I'll start with the Jewish religious history and prove to you that you're a hoax and that I'm fine.

> *But Jesus wasn't there to talk religion nor argue about rules; He was simply there for relationship.*

But Jesus wasn't there to talk about religion or argue rules. He was there for a relationship. Mistakenly, she thought that Jesus was like many other men she had encountered, just there to get something *from* her, when He had come to give something *to* her. Away from His own people, Jesus had come specifically to meet with her. He sought her out and spoke to her soul, longing to set her life on a completely new course.

We can't blame her for being skeptical. She'd been playing the games of religion and relationship, yet never winning was exhausting. She was tired of the cycle. She basically asked Jesus, *What's in this for me?*

Control gets really good at manipulating the external trauma but has little power over the internal turmoil. Drawing water was a necessary part of life and one thing the Samaritan woman could control.

I've been there. My *No.thing* gave me a false sense of security—something I could hold on to as mine. Living in fear for most of my life, I felt like I was essentially saving myself from danger and hardship. I feared the known and feared the unknown. Feared the old and feared the new. Feared the now and feared the next. I wouldn't admit it was fear and didn't recognize it as such. I thought I was controlling disappointment, but internally, I was a messed-up wreck.

> The issue is fear. But the deeper issue is trust. Can we trust our lives, our futures, and the lives of those we love to God? Can we trust a God we can't control? Can we trust this God whose take on life and death and suffering and joy is so very different from our own? Yes. Yes, we can because we know him. And we know he is good. — Stasi Eldredge [1]

The driving factor of this woman's fear and anxiousness was that she was missing something and couldn't figure out exactly what it was. She was searching for a *thing*, not a person.

While her thirst had been quenched by the world, her soul was parched. Her arms were full, yet her heart was empty.

> "Sir, give me this water so that I won't get thirsty and have to keep coming here to draw water." (John 4:15 NIV)

Jesus was different than any other human she had ever encountered. He wasn't seeking control. He wanted communion. He wasn't challenging religion. He was interested in restoration. And while she focused on all of the external problems, Jesus pegged her internal issue of relinquishing control in exchange for living water.

I can relate to this Samaritan woman—juggling and fighting for control of my little water pot, struggling with my *No.thing*, while Jesus stands there offering to swap it for His *everything*. Jesus saw my control-based issue of fear and offered to exchange for faith.

Just like the woman at the well, when I dared to believe that less of me and more of Him would bring complete satisfaction, it was the *next* for me. And when I let go of the thing I clung on to and began trusting God to work all things out for me, it was transformational.

This section of your life, the one with *No.thing*, can be the catalyst to a breakthrough, one that begins inside of you. It can't help but to spill out.

We see it in the next picture of this woman. As Jesus melts her heart of distrust, she leaves her jar sitting on the well and runs to tell the entire village about the new thing Jesus was about to do.

> Then, leaving her water jar, the woman went back to
> the town and said to the people, "Come, see a man
> who told me everything I ever did. Could this be the
> Messiah?" (John 4:29-29 NIV)

In that moment, none of the questions of religion mattered to her. She stopped asking Jesus where His jar was because she saw what He could do.

As our *No.thing* pales in comparison to the new thing that Jesus has offered to us, we, too, will go—like Jacque and like the woman at the well, we'll tell everyone we know. This Man has been so good to me!"

Digging Deeper

- How does self-preservation hinder me spiritually?

- When do I recognize control issues showing up in my life?

- Have disappointments shaped me into a different person than God intends for me to be? How can I remedy this?

- What does the water jar represent in my life?

_____

_____

_____

_____

_____

_____

_____

10

Googling ... but Nothing Helpful Pops Up

Wisdom is knowing what to do next; virtue is doing it.
—David Starr Jordan

Every evening, I spent time watering my plants and front lawn and watched as a neighbor left her house for work. My heart tugged at me, and I felt God saying more to me. But I didn't want to hear. So instead of obeying, I casually waved as she drove by.

The internal dialogue intensified a few days later, when God told me to go over to her house and speak to her. But I didn't know what to say. So instead, I put her on my urgent prayer list and hoped that would suffice.

Early one morning, God again abruptly spoke two words to me: *"Chocolate pie."*

I rebutted, *"but* does she even like chocolate? *But* what if she hates pie?"

"Just take her the pie," God said.

I can imagine Him giving me an eye roll right then.

After giving a bunch of reasons and excuses not to obey, I finally did. Using what was in my house and hand, I took over the pie and spoke to my neighbor for the very first time. Should I have been at all surprised when she grabbed me in a bear hug and told me how she desperately needed a friend? How did God know? Working all night at a hustler club left her sad and depleted; googling an answer wouldn't have helped her. She needed me to share the oil of gladness and the love of Jesus with my chocolate pie. By resisting, I almost missed a momentous occurrence for her and me.

Here, in the "less than" neighborhood I told you about earlier, Jesus had strategically placed me to spread the good news of the gospel. It begins with me, you, us!

Doing that next thing, whatever God asks us to do, revalues our *No.thing* into something much greater.

Notice this story given to us in the Bible. She didn't ask to become a single mom, providing for her two young sons with no income, no supporting relatives, and no hope of marrying again. After the death of her husband, paying the bills became impossible. Working online from home wasn't even a thing. Googling for help was non-existent, yet life had to go on.

Some may call it weak or breaking down to ask for help; she had no other option. Her story goes like this:

> Now the wife of one of the sons of the prophets cried out to Elisha, "Your servant, my husband, is dead, and you know that your servant feared the LORD. And now his creditor is coming to take my two children as his slaves!" "How can I help you?" asked Elisha. "Tell me, what do you have in the house?"
>
> She answered, "Your servant has *nothing* in the house *but* a jar of oil."
>
> "Go," said Elisha, "borrow jars, even empty ones, from all your neighbors. Do not gather just a few. Then go inside, shut the door behind you and

your sons, and pour oil into all these jars, setting the full ones aside."

So she left him, and after she had shut the door behind her and her sons, they kept bringing jars to her, and she kept pouring. When all the jars were full, she said to her son, "Bring me another."

But he replied, "There are no more jars." Then the oil stopped flowing.

She went and told the man of God, and he said, "Go, sell the oil, and pay your debt. Then you and your sons can live on the remainder." (2 Kings 4:1-7, emphasis mine)

Beginning with her *No.thing*, this lady first had to kick *but* to the curb and recognize the possibility of what was directly under her roof. Then she had to collect all the empty containers from all of her neighbors. Finally, she sold the oil to pay off debts.

God chose to work through what this woman had at that *very* moment within *her* possession. Her story strongly depicts the theme of this book. The miracle often is in our hands and takes place when we believe and do the next thing by pouring from the oil flask that we previously have called a *No.thing*.

Can you hear His voice asking:

What is in your house?

What is in your heart?

What is in your hand?

For Moses, it was a shepherd's staff that God used to perform miracles; he spread it over a giant sea, rolling it back so God's people could walk through. With this same staff, he struck a rock in the desert and water poured forth for over a million people.

For Chip and Angela, it was a loving home. They waited almost a decade with nothing in the womb. By going outside of their own hurting hearts, they found two other little hearts who desperately needed a family to love and adopt them.

For Becky, it was a mop. She dared to answer the question, *what is in your hand?* She took that mop, added a broom and a bucket, and started her own cleaning company.

For my friend Johnnie Lynn, it means giving out smiles to everyone she meets. "We shall never know all the good that a simple smile can do" (Mother Teresa).

For Danny and Lindsi, it meant opening up a small vegan restaurant that employs teenagers from all walks of society and ethnicity, giving them an opportunity and a work ethic they would not have had otherwise. When God asked, "What is in your house?" this couple not only opened their hands and heart but also their beautiful home with empty rooms and filled it with foster teens who needed a home, a job, and a lot of love.

For me, it was nothing but a ballpoint pen. For over two years, God nudged me to write this book. I felt like I had nothing to say, nothing to offer, nothing you would want to hear. I struggled to put myself out there to write these words. Painstakingly, I took what was in my hand and wrote the things from my heart as a journal entry ... and then wrote another and another.

I'm sitting out in my lawn chair crying through my sunglasses as I finally say this to you, because those dreams He plants within our souls are SO much more than a *No.thing*. Dare I say, they are a God-thing! We just need to leverage our nothing by leaping into His everything.

Barriers, unbelief, and *trouble* will no longer keep us down or impede our progress. Obedience is the key. You may be standing there like the woman in our story with a flask of oil that's almost dry, or you might even be questioning (like I did over the chocolate pie) if anyone wants what you have to offer. It's a barrier. The thing you have prayed for and desired may be long overdue and unbelief has seeped in. Maybe the trouble has been so great that you don't care enough to try again. Go ahead and say it with me—it's time to kick *but* to the curb!

I promise you that when God adds His *something* to your *nothing*, the oil of His Spirit will begin to flow supernaturally from your vessel into the vessels of your entire community. Don't shy away from the question of what is in your hand because we are the hands and feet of Jesus, doing His work here on this earth—not our work, *His* work.

You need more than a three-second Google answer. I want you to dig deeper into the dream or desire God planted inside of you and prayerfully ask yourself and God these three questions: What is in my house? What is in my heart? What is in my hand? And then go out and do what God tells you to do!

Digging Deeper

- When was the last time I felt the call to something bigger than myself?
- How has the barrier, unbelief, or trouble of *No.thing* hindered my God-given dream?
- Which of those three questions—heart, house, hand—speaks to me the most?
- In what way do I feel prompted to obey?
- What action step will I take today?

_____

_____

_____

_____

_____

Section Three

New thing

11

Breaking Free

But forget all that—
*   it is **nothing** compared to what I am going to do.*
*For I am about to do **something new**. See, I have already*
*   begun! Do you not see it?*
I will make a pathway through the wilderness.
*   I will create rivers in the dry wasteland.*

—Isaiah 43:18-19 NLT, emphasis mine

Do butterflies feel weird when they emerge from their chrysalis?

Let's really think about the anatomy of a caterpillar vs. butterfly for a second. While the head, thorax and abdomen are relatively the same, everything else drastically changes. Stubby fleshy foot-like prolegs turn into wispy feathery-like legs with a femur, tibia, and tarsus. A new normal is the afterlife of a caterpillar, and I just can't help but wonder if it feels a little abnormal.

Coming out of quarantine because of a global pandemic, we all related to being cramped, restricted, and cooped up. Solidarity and isolation look like a wasteland when we are in the middle; it just does. And those on the outside may not see anything going on inside of us, but good things transpire there.

Transformation is much more than behavior modification or alteration. More than changing an outward image, it implies a change of character and little or no resemblance with the past configuration or structure. No matter who we are, change requires a crisis-like experience of complete reformation.

His name was on a federal most-wanted list for white-collar crime. As president and CEO of a large credit union, he generated millions of dollars legitimately, but his runaway greed spun out of control. Excessive and fraudulent loans provided him with a small fleet of vehicles (including a red Ferrari), a lavish 9,000-square-foot mansion, a plane, and properties worth over $20 million.

Busted: A Banker's Run to Prison describes the life of Richard D. Mangone and his acts of white-collar crime. He had it all—everything money could buy. "Yet," he wrote, "even with all that wealth, I was still empty inside, always seeking the next score or hit." He hoodwinked everyone for many years until national auditors finally uncovered the illegal dealings of conspiracy and fraud. Running from his criminal behavior, Richard left the big city and hid in the hills of Tennessee.

Landing himself on the U.S. Marshals' most-wanted-fugitives list, Richard was at the end of his rope and made plans to end his life. Miraculously, through a television evangelist, he met Jesus. A new thing was created inside of him, and he stopped running from himself and the authorities by turning himself in.

After serving his time in prison, Richard gave this testimony: "Prison gave me the opportunity to grow in Christ and to finally become the person God wanted me to be. I hope to minister to as many prisoners as I can, especially white-collar criminals who are so susceptible to attempting suicide. What remains of my life is dedicated to the Lord's work. I'm at peace now, enjoying the fruits of helping others."[1]

Transformation into a new thing is slow and painful like metamorphosis; necessary and time-consuming, yet so rewarding. The cocooning process is hidden away from busyness, giving us space to change, grow, and mature.

In an organizational context, transformation is a process of profound change that orients it in a new direction and takes it to an entirely different level of effectiveness. In the case of the butterfly, this stage of development could appear fatal while hanging suspended in mid-air. Scientists tell us that during this life-cycle process, the body tissues of the caterpillar are completely reorganized to produce the beautiful adult butterfly that emerges from the pupa (or chrysalis). Inside the pupa, the caterpillar actually turns to liquid as it transforms into a butterfly. [2]

You may feel like your insides are mush as you hang upside down, but if the isolated place is where God is taking you, do not be alarmed. It's all a part of breaking you free. Don't worry. You will fly soon.

Over a cup of coffee, my friend Stacey relayed her experience of transition. As she spilled her story of their move from a town, church, and career they had been happy and comfortable in, I saw the title *No.thing* and the four sections of this book vividly shining through her testimony.

Working prior to the move as an oncology nurse, she had found fulfillment in a busy and successful career. On Sundays, she was a worship leader for her church and found purpose in music ministry with her local community of believers. When her husband's practice transferred across the country, it uprooted everything. Gone was the private school for the kids, her career, and beloved worship ministry. She had felt stripped to *No.thing* and was tempted to look back at the former things God had done.

Instead, she grew and stretched, broke through skins of comfort, and accepted change. She obeyed and followed the leading of providence by doing the next thing God asked her to do. And in the midst of hanging seemingly upside down, a new thing was being done inside of her.

She now says, "I've become aware that God is breaking me free of trusting in my own comfort zone and asking me to trust more fully and entirely in Him."

Nature has something to teach us here about forgetting the old things and anticipating the new thing God is doing. Becoming a new thing might first be similar to a monarch caterpillar that molts several times before it even reaches the chrysalis stage. The exoskeleton gives strength to the body and is, therefore, imperative, yet it is composed of *chitin,* which is dead matter and incapable of growing as the caterpillar does. To keep up the growth process, the caterpillar must accommodate the increase of size by growing a new layer of chitin and then shedding the dead outer layer.

Here is the point I want us to catch: The new layer is soft and stretchy, while the outer layer is hard and crusty. In order to grow, we have to be willing to stretch and to shed that outer layer that has given us protection far too long. We can't be afraid to shed off the old to become new.

> *In order to grow us, we have to be willing to stretch and to shed that outer layer that has given us protection far too long. We can't be afraid to shed off the old to become new.*

For years, God tried to break me free and give me a new identity, but I was afraid to shed the outer layer of security that had become my reality. My layer was fear. I was afraid to be trapped and afraid to be free. I was fearful of having too little and fearful of having too much. Afraid to say yes and afraid to say no. Fearful of the seen and fearful of the unseen. Afraid to live in my now and afraid to step into my next. And while my exoskeleton protected me from the outside, it prohibited me from growing on the inside. God called me out on it by telling me that my superficial security had been fortified with fear in place of faith. Then He challenged me to stretch like never before to grow a new skin.

Flying Isn't Always Comfortable

I married my high school sweetheart a few months before my 19th birthday. All the wedding details were arranged by me, and all the surprising destinations and excursions of our honeymoon were left to him.

As we wound our way through the beautiful Ozark mountains, we finally stopped at our next excursion of the day. "Here we are," my new hubby said with excitement as he parked the car and turned the ignition off. We made our way over to a ticket booth with an orange windsock flapping in the air. A sign stood nearby with big box letters that read, "$50 Helicopter Rides." I took a deep breath and tried to remain calm.

Jay's eyes were dancing as he reached for my hand and said, "I've always wanted to ride a helicopter! Isn't this going to be fun?"

As a kid, I had dreamed of flying the cloudless skies, but as an adult, I had nightmares of my feet flying unsecured through the air. Somehow, it just didn't seem safe. I tried to tell him that he could go ahead and I would wait. But how do you dash the dreams of your new husband?

> New layers of growth don't just happen. We choose to grow on purpose. That day I grew a new layer of faith by stepping through my fear.

I climbed up and in, strapped the seat belt on, and placed the headset on my ears. Surviving the lift-off, I finally managed to breathe normally and opened my eyes again in an attempt to view the scenery. The fatal mistake was peering down as we hovered over the deep water-filled gorge and canyon. My heart left me at first glance, I saw nothing under my feet but a glass bubble, and immediately my stomach felt sick. Jay then gasped and exclaimed through the earpiece, "Esther, isn't this gorgeous?"

Flying comes at a price. If I wanted to see the beautiful sights, I'd have to swallow my comfort. New layers of growth don't just happen. We choose to grow on purpose. That day I grew a new layer of faith by stepping through my fear.

Breaking free in who God meant me to be was definitely a molting and cocooning type of experience—so much change had to happen on the inside of me before anyone saw a difference on the outside.

Stretching may look like trusting God through the growing pains of something new and strange. New things are just that— new! Sometimes they're a little weird and sometimes a lot scary. Think about it. Caterpillars crawl inch by inch, safely, slowly, and meticulously—eating leaves of plants, flowers, or fruits. But butterflies break free by flapping wings, spinning, and soaring through the air. It all becomes new.

You may be asking, I get the butterfly story, but what does breaking free look like for me? Isaiah 43:18-19 puts it like this,

> Forget the former things;
>> do not dwell on the past.
> See, I am doing a *new thing*!
>> Now it springs up; do you not perceive it?
> I am making a way in the wilderness
>> and streams in the wasteland. (NIV)

Based on the foundational truths of this verse, I'll give you these three hacks to breaking free:

- **Forget it.** Forget the wrong that was done to you. Forget the old you. Forget the mistakes. Forget the hurt. Forget what "could have been." So many people get stuck right here in the could-have, would-have, should-have trap. Forget it and move on.

- **Don't dwell on it.** Forget the former things. Put an end to obsessing over past memories and choose to actively live in the present moment. Time is ticking. Going back is not an option. Trade in your past for today.

- **See!** Before skipping over to the words "new thing," grasp this truth: *I am* doing a new thing. *I am* making a way. Jesus is the focus. See Him, the way maker, instead of looking for a perfect way. New things "spring up" where you least expect them—even in the wilderness.

Breaking free takes effort on our part, but the joy of finding fulfillment in Christ far outweighs the struggle. I don't know about you, but I don't ever want to fully return to a life that I used to call "normal." The new normal that God is bringing us into is not going to send us back to normalcy. If the hard place is where He is taking you, do not be alarmed. Trust and obey Him. We can't be afraid of the new thing God is doing inside of us because dramatic transformation is going to feel different. Be different.

Don't turn back and long to munch on the juicy green leaves of the past; you are no longer a caterpillar. Sure, we remember former days of growth as part of the necessary cycle to get us to where we are today, but we don't dwell there.

See! Take a peek at the new you emerging as a beautifully developed butterfly that drinks nectar and flies. So break free, my friend, feel the wind beneath your wings and fly!

Digging Deeper

- Do new things excite me or worry me?
- What comforts in my own life prevent me from growing?
- How do I see myself, flying or crawling? Eating leaves or drinking nectar?
- What is one thing I feel God is prompting me to "shed" or change?

_____

_____

_____

_____

_____

_____

_____

12

Nothing Wrong with Nothing

If our identity is in our work, rather than Christ, success will go to our heads, and failure will go to our hearts.

— Timothy Keller

From the beginning of time, man has encountered nothing—but at first, the *No.thing* was a good thing. We find perfection in the human forms of Adam and Eve, created in the very image of God (Gen. 1:26-27). Without blemish. Perfect. Whole. Complete. Nothing broken and nothing missing. Beautiful and majestic in naked unashamed splendor, dressed in God's righteousness alone. "Adam and his wife were both naked, and they felt no shame" (Gen. 2:25).

But their perfect world was marred when sin entered the garden and stole their hearts, along with their trust in God. "When the woman saw that the fruit of the tree was good for food and pleasing to the eye, and also desirable for gaining wisdom, she took some and ate it. She also gave some to her husband, who was with her, and he ate it. Then the eyes of both of them were opened, and they realized they were naked; so they sewed fig leaves together and made coverings for themselves" (Gen. 3:6-7 NIV).

For the first time, they viewed *No.thing* as a "condition" and quickly worked to cover up.

From that day until now, humanity has worked feverishly and sewn-together fig leaves of our own making. Dressing ourselves in wealth and luxury, we take on garments of honor and praise. Embellishing ourselves with roles and status. Adding titles and degrees. Dazzling up with beauty tips and power tricks.

These are all futile attempts to hide the *No.thing* buried deep within.

Sin, society, and self encourage us to cover the nothing, to hide and stifle it. But *what if* we could realize the freedom of once again being naked and open before our living Creator?

And what if *No.thing* turns out to be the greatest blessing a person could have?

See, I really believe it's time to peel back *all* the layers and *all* of the baggage and garbage draped around us and upon us. It's past time to throw it off and discover what was there in the very beginning.

Simply people and their Maker.

Nothing more, nothing less.

The early believers found new life in Christ yet struggled with their new identity. While the old laws, ways, and traditions changed, some still clung to their own efforts, a *thing* to grasp, and applied undue pressure upon the new Christians to do the same. The Apostle Paul was disturbed and wrote these words, "After starting your new lives in the Spirit, why are you now trying to become perfect by your own human effort? Have you experienced so much for *nothing*?" (Gal. 3:3-4 NLT, emphasis mine). Salvation by grace alone was under attack in the churches at Galatia, and the same faction of division is used today.

We are our biggest critics. Yet our value is not determined by other people's opinions about us, neither is it measured by the scrutiny of ourselves. You are loved for who you are (and may I emphasize, *whose* you are), not for what you do.

It's time we, as image-bearers of our Creator, fully know who God has created us to be—living out our full design—our purpose, not merely showing off potential, living in pretense or striving for perfection. Maybe you have it all put together on the outside, but your insides are pulling apart.

> You are loved for who you are (and may I emphasize, whose you are) not for what you do.

You think you are a no thing. That's why you depend on things, titles, accolades, and money. But you *are* something. You are worthy. You are the created (Ps. 139:14). The redeemed (Eph. 1:7). The chosen (1 Pet. 2). Sons and daughters (Gal. 4). Heirs (Rom. 8). Family (Gal. 3:26).

There's nothing wrong with you. You need nothing but what you already have—Father who loves you, adores you, has your hairs numbered, and has your days counted. He's made paths in the wilderness and streams in the desert (Isa. 43). He fights for you and with you (Exod. 14). He goes behind you and before you. He shaped you and formed you (Ps. 139). He has plans with you and promises for you (Jer. 29:11).

The enemy yells lies that you have no royal blood. You have no armies. You are *nothing*!!!

We take a small portion of that lie into ourselves, as if ownership brings kinship. Without God, we *are* nothing. But *with* Him ... we are everything! And that's the truth of the whole matter. My nothing actually gives space and grace for my Creator to become something within me, and through me, *all* things are indeed possible.

See, the enemy doesn't want us naked and open. He wants us to be shrouded with all the trappings of this world. And if that trick doesn't work, he will then either point at our little bony bodies or poke at our big stocky beings, causing us to once again scramble for leaves in an attempt to cover up our *No.thing*.

In this condition, we begin to view ourselves as "stripped" to nothing, as Satan then accuses us, tempting us to doubt our true belonging, identity, and authority.

Yet all the while, we are the King's sons and daughters. We are His feet, His hands, His mouth—created by Him to bring forth much fruit. We are called, loved, adored, chosen.

So let's be honest and open about the nothing we feel, the nothing we see, and the nothing creeping up inside of us. We won't ever find what we are seeking inside our own security. That thing we search for to have a meaningful life—the thing that drives us forward, where we just want to find our purpose is only found in the place of authenticity by embracing our identity in Christ.

Authenticity is an intimidating word that purely means being real and true. It's nothing more than being vulnerable, exposed, naked—just me and my God, walking together in communion. I ask myself, and now you, *Do you long to live in God's presence with authenticity, unashamed with nothing on*? I sure do, and that flat-out scares the enemy!

So run free in who you were meant to be, with nothing on but Him! Leverage your nothing to something by leaping into his everything. I invite you to meditate on this psalm and remind yourself Whose you are:

You Know All About Me

Lord, you know everything there is to know about
  me.
You perceive every movement of my heart and soul,
  and you understand my every thought before it
  even enters my mind.
You are so intimately aware of me, Lord.
  You read my heart like an open book
  and you know all the words I'm about to speak
  before I even start a sentence!

You know every step I will take before my journey even begins.
You've gone into my future to prepare the way,
and in kindness you follow behind me
to spare me from the harm of my past.
You have laid your hand on me!
This is just too wonderful, deep, and incomprehensible! Your understanding of me brings me wonder and strength.
Where could I go from your Spirit?
Where could I run and hide from your face?
If I go up to heaven, you're there!
If I go down to the realm of the dead, you're there too!
If I fly with wings into the shining dawn, you're there! If I fly into the radiant sunset, you're there waiting!
Wherever I go, your hand will guide me;
your strength will empower me.
It's impossible to disappear from you
or to ask the darkness to hide me,
for your presence is everywhere, bringing light into my night.
There is no such thing as darkness with you.
The night, to you, is as bright as the day;
there's no difference between the two.
You formed my innermost being, shaping my delicate inside
and my intricate outside,
and wove them all together in my mother's womb.
I thank you, God, for making me so mysteriously complex! Everything you do is marvelously breathtaking.

It simply amazes me to think about it!
How thoroughly you know me, Lord!
You even formed every bone in my body
    when you created me in the secret place,
    carefully, skillfully shaping me from *nothing* to
    something.
You saw who you created me to be before I became
    me! Before I'd ever seen the light of day,
    the number of days you planned for me
    were already recorded in your book. (Ps. 139:1-16
    TPT, emphasis mine)

Digging Deeper

- How has *No.thing* made me feel "less than"?

- Does striving for perfection work for me or hinder my mission?

- How does society put undue pressure on me to perform?

- What "thing" am I seeking in hopes of fulfillment?

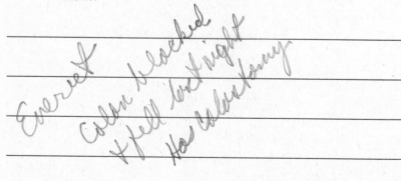

13

You Ain't Seen Nothing Yet!

*Start by doing what's necessary; then do what's possible;
and suddenly you are doing the impossible.*

—Francis of Assisi

I love when a good guy finally wins and has enough guts to smart off to those who have been talking smack. This plot twist is probably one of my favorites, which is crazy because I never intended to go here with this book. But I'm on this journey with you and feel God is still speaking to our hearts. So after writing the previous chapter, this one totally fits. Here we go!

David was the young shepherd boy with a sling who defied and killed the giant Goliath. He was still a kid at the time, bringing lunch to his brothers who were pretending at war (1 Sam. 17). Being at the right place at the right time, he overhears Goliath smack-talking his God, and it was game on! Courageously, David fought and Goliath fell, while the entire Israelite army hid in their tents (1 Sam. 17:24). The moment this Philistine's body came crashing to the ground in defeat, the war for Israel was won. The king and all of Israel had seen nothing like this before. David had gone viral. Instantly, all the women were creating new *TikToks* about Saul killing his thousands and David killing 10 thousands.

As promised to the man who heroically killed Goliath, King Saul's daughter Michal was given to David in marriage.

But things took a turn. David's increased victories as a mighty warrior compounded his popularity among the people and infuriated the jealous king, who became determined to kill David. Fortunately, Michal received intel from her father's palace and helped David escape for his life. In an act of revenge, Saul retrieved his daughter, David's wife, and gave her to another man. Commentators agree that Saul's giving Michal to Phalti was intended to signal the final rupture of his own relations with David by marking the completeness of the breach between them. And so David spent the next several miserable years dodging an unhinged king, hiding in damp, dark caves and fearing for his life.

By the time we reach the portion of David's story we are to focus on, God has rejected Saul as king of Israel and the prophet Samuel has anointed David to replace him. After realizing the loss of God's blessing, Saul dies by his own sword on the battlefield. And David is exulted. Once on the throne, King David gets his wife back, and he restores the ark of God to its rightful place in Israel:

> And David danced before the Lord with all his might, wearing a priestly garment [a linen ephod]. So David and all the people of Israel brought up the Ark of the Lord with shouts of joy and the blowing of rams' horns. (2 Sam. 6:14-15 NLT)

Notice Michal's contempt for David:

> But as the Ark of the Lord entered the City of David, Michal, the daughter of Saul, looked down from her window. When she saw King David leaping and

dancing before the Lord, she was filled with contempt for him.

They brought the Ark of the Lord and set it in its place inside the special tent David had prepared for it. And David sacrificed burnt offerings and peace offerings to the Lord. When he had finished his sacrifices, David blessed the people in the name of the Lord of Heaven's Armies. Then he gave to every Israelite man and woman in the crowd a loaf of bread, a cake of dates, and a cake of raisins. Then all the people returned to their homes. (2 Sam. 6:16-19 NLT)

Capture Michal's scorn for David:

When David returned home to bless his own family, Michal, the daughter of Saul, came out to meet him. She said in disgust, "How distinguished the king of Israel looked today, shamelessly exposing himself to the servant girls like any vulgar person might do!" (2 Sam. 6:20 NLT)

See David's slap-bang response in freedom of worship:

David retorted to Michal, "I was dancing before the Lord, who chose me above your father and all his family! He appointed me as the leader of Israel, the people of the Lord, so I celebrate before the Lord. Yes, and I am willing to look even more foolish than this, even to be humiliated in my own eyes!" (2 Sam. 6:21-22a NLT)

In other words, if you think this is bad. Just wait. I'm willing to disgrace myself even more. Michal talked smack and just got whacked.

David wanted nothing more than to glorify a God who had shown Himself strong on behalf of this little shepherd boy who had been hunted through the wilderness like a wild animal. One who suffers much rejoices much. New things had come, causing David to dance and leap in unfettered gratitude to the Lord who had defeated all his enemies.

Forgetting entirely about himself, King David praised and worshipped with all pretense of power put aside. In the presence of God, he responded in complete reverence and humility. David stripped himself of everything else. His gown and crown were thrown off, sword and scepter cast to the side—nothing of the kingly garb remained.

Michal despised a husband who danced before the Lord as a commoner. She preferred to be shrouded in all of her glory. Michal didn't get it. She could have joined in on the celebration but sat angrily gazing out the window at a God-honoring king.

Criticism will come as we begin to shed the worldly garments of pride, power, prestige, and prejudice; our nakedness will either offend or inspire people.

> **Val·ue** *noun*
> 1. the regard that something is held to deserve; the importance, worth, or usefulness of something.
> 2. a person's principles or standards of behavior; one's judgment of what is important in life.

In a world desperate to validate one's self-worth, we feel like we need a "thing" to prove our value—desperately struggling to find purpose in our life by being something that proves our success by doing or saying something significant. That's why, like Michal, we really don't want to be associated with anything that resembles a *No.thing*.

David's identity wasn't misplaced in the importance of his role or who he was in the eyes of the world, but who he was in Christ. He was not depending upon his title *as* king but rested in his relationship as a child *of* the King. Whether a lowly shepherd sitting on a grassy green hill or a king on a red velvet throne,

David's value was deeply rooted in the Lord alone. Not a mocking giant nor contentious wife could take him down.

David was confident and knew *who* he was. He knew that he was a warrior, musician, communicator, leader, and king. But more importantly, he was secure in knowing *whose* he was.

Long ago, this musician by trade had established this relationship while watching sheep and strumming a harp. He was a soulful being, communicating spirit to spirit with his God in an unrestricted expression of singing and playing a melody. David grew up free-spirited as an unrestricted teen, writing songs, treating himself kindly, and loving his creator. This kid wasn't afraid to face a lion, bear, or giant, yet he had to grow up overnight when fame came to him unexpectedly. He hadn't asked for honor or a king's robe, and while he respected what it stood for, no amount of power or position could thwart his first love.

> *All you need to accomplish God's purpose in your life is God's permission and approval—not anyone else's.*

All you need to accomplish God's purpose in your life is God's permission and approval, not anyone else's.

Like David, I want to be okay in my own skin with nothing else to validate me but God. Don't you? I want to live a life of worship, whether that is through my current job or through serving my family and community. I want to live a life of nothing but Him—refusing to be tied to anyone else's standards of orientation, denomination, or notion. Do you want the same?

Trust me. *No.thing* fits good on you too! And I have a feeling we ain't seen nothin' yet!

Digging Deeper

- How do you praise the Lord for His goodness to you?

- What exactly does becoming vulnerable in worship look like for you?

- Does your sense of self-worth affect your worship?

- Have the opinions of others stunted your freedom of worship?

- Is your best worship vocal or quiet? Private and/or public?

_____

_____

_____

_____

_____

_____

_____

_____

14

Grit, Spit, & Grin

I prayed for 20 years but received no answer until I prayed with my legs.

—Frederick Douglass

There I stood outfitted in a school gym uniform—pencil-thin bird legs tucked inside gray suede tennis shoes with a light pink checkmark on the side. My hand clutched a wooden bat that had been placed there by my PE teacher. I firmly believed that my previous performance problem was an equipment issue, that my bat was inferior. I wanted the aluminum one I had just watched the last player use to score a homerun. That was it. Convinced I needed a different bat, I threw the wooden bat down and picked up the aluminum one. It was heavier than I anticipated, but I was determined to use this lucky bat and win.

"Strike one!"

The umpire's voice brought me back to reality.

Visions of once again striking out caused me to wince. I was typically one of those last-picked players, always standing against a fence line waiting my turn.

"Strike two!" he yelled.

Silently, I wondered if I should spit on my hands to help things along. The bases were loaded; it was up to me. If I failed, we would be forced to the outfield and our team would lose.

"Keep your eye on the ball," I heard the captain yelling. And then, all I remember is a ball coming straight for me. With determination, I hit it as hard as I could.

"Run, run, run!" they cried as I barreled forward. My ball flew straight for first base, but the catcher missed, which saved me from an automatic out. Invigorated by renewed adrenaline, I ran as hard as I could. My foot was inches away from touching first base when I felt the glove tag my hip. I was out. But I felt like a winner as everyone cheered because my play had gotten all three players ahead of me home!

Hear me. Just because you are out for this play doesn't mean that the game is over. You're part of a bigger picture, and your team is counting on you to make the hit and give it all you've got. That day my team scored three points from my play because I gritted and sprinted.

This is exactly what it means to leverage our *No.thing*, because we serve a God who acts in multiples, groups, and teams. With him, our little becomes more. Although I was hitting on my own up at the batter's box, I was not *all* alone; I was not the only player but part of a team. You and I aren't on a solo mission—we are part of God's team. *"We are laborers together with God"* (1 Cor. 1:9 KJV). In other words, we are not the "all-star player" in this thing because it's not all about me—it's all about *us*!!

Activating the Bigger Play

I was a Gen X baby, one of those who grew up constructing life-size mazes out of cardboard boxes and building tents in the living room using flat and fitted sheets and every other blanket in the linen closet. I remember climbing trees with a bag carefully strapped around my shoulders, finding a brown knobby branch to plop down on, and reading under a high leafy canopy. Computers and cell phones were non-existent, but our generation didn't lack for activity, and we knew better than to say the words, "I'm bored."

Our summer days were filled to the brim with imagination. We played library, placing hand-stamped pieces of carefully torn paper cards into every single book found in our tall family bookcase. I was the "nice" librarian and wore thick, black-framed 80s-style glasses that made me go cross-eyed. Oh, and I can't forget about the straightened paper clip I strung across my teeth as a mock braces' retainer (which was to die for in those days. Does anyone else remember the 1980s orthodontic headgear?).

I've read that Gen-X people have grit; they know how to create something out of basically nothing. My sister and I got really good at adapting supplies to make things work, like using black shoe polish for mascara or toothpaste to scrub the grouted tile around the bathroom sink. I recall finding real bandages in a friend's medicine cabinet. At my house, we used tissue and scotch tape.

I started out tough and gritty. My motto has always been, if the dog doesn't have a tail to wag, then let's make him one and pin it on. Then life hit me full force, and my *No.thing* took the wind right out of my sails. As storms brewed, the mental battles became intense. I had to dig deep within and grit some things out.

Grit isn't necessarily a generational or personality trait, but it is a spiritual practice we can form. It's one thing to recognize a new thing God is doing inside of us and quite another to implement daily habits that support that new way of living. *"Whether you eat or drink, or whatever you do, do it all for the glory of God"* (1 Cor. 10:31).

Those of you who are naturally wired to push through tough things and adapt, I get that you want to power through the hard days and get to the good days. I bet you didn't read the first half of the book before skipping to this chapter. I see you. But you have to promise to go back and read the beginning of this book to fully benefit.

To others of you, who are grit type of people yet need some time to methodically process every word and enjoy the journey, the following action steps are here for you.

When life throws you a curveball, sometimes there's no good explanation. This list of five life hacks is a simple guide to help lighten your mood and keep you free in spirit. It's one to highlight, post on your fridge or bathroom mirror:

1. Grip
2. Hit
3. Grit
4. Spit
5. Grin

First, *grip* onto what God has given to you—whatever is in your hand will work. Get your eyes off your problem (the bat isn't your issue) and set them back onto the goal. The ball is coming! Stop stressing about your *No.thing* and get ready to swing.

Hit! For my go-getter reader, here's a little caution. Not every ball is your ball. Don't swing at every opportunity. Some pitches are just foul balls—don't waste your energy on them. Lysa Terkeurst in her book, *The Best Yes*, says, "Find that courageous *yes*. Fight for that confident *no*." Choose what is best for you, for your family, for your situation and have confidence in that choice. Choose and then hit your hardest, knowing that you made the best decision possible in that moment.

Grit and power through the extremely difficult seasons. Take one day, one moment, one task at a time. Put some muscle into it. Sweat a little, cry a little, and don't complain if others don't come help as quickly as you think they should. Grit it out.

Spit out the dust, sand, hurt feelings or whatever annoyance is grinding in your teeth. Commit your works to the Lord (Prov. 16:3). Be determined not to quit. You may be asking, so why the spit? I purposely left it in this chapter because I've found that some situations are dirty, messy, and there's no other way around it but to spit and go on.

Grin: Be kind enough to laugh at yourself. We all make mistakes. None of us is perfect, and hindsight is always a truer picture. This step is probably the most or equally important. It's one I haven't yet mastered, but I'm trying hard, and so far, it's really working! Grinning is imperative to becoming new. It involves shedding the old garments of negativity and self-deprivation by developing positivity and affirmation. We are still growing.

I'll tell on myself one more time. Sigh! Grinning at my foolishness has always been difficult. For most of my adult life, I've lived with a pessimistic slant. I honestly thought I was born that way, and for many years fought to preserve my way of dealing with things because I thought it was beneficial in saving me from disappointment. But God started nudging me about my outlook and, hence, the title of this book—*No.thing*. He began to show me that what I saw as a *no thing* could actually be a *new thing* when placed in His hands.

Now, I'm a total believer in this concept of transitioning to joyful maturity. It might take me a lifetime to master it, yet mastery isn't the goal here. Living is. Living free in who I was meant to be. Living in the moment. Living and shifting, renaming, and reframing. Living while spitting and grinning. Living a life of showing others what freedom in Christ really is. Do you see it? We were created to live in grit *and* grin.

We have to do our best and place the rest into God's hands. We have to play and run our hardest. Keeping our eyes on the goal. Sure, we might struggle on the plays in this game of life, but for those who have put our trust in Him, we all win someday. Heaven is the real goal!

God is preparing for us that special place, but here in real-time life leading up to eternity, you've got to grip firmly on the promises of God as He creates a new thing around you and inside of you. Leap into His everything. Hit the good times and revel in the joy of them, remembering that green grass requires dirt to grow in and life gets dry, dusty, and dirty sometimes.

So if you need to, go ahead and spit along the way. I won't tell. But don't you dare forget to grin.

Digging Deeper

Take a moment and answer in your own words the following questions based upon the five-step life hack introduced in this chapter. Then go ahead and personalize that action template for your mirror:

- What is in my grip, and am I using it to the best of my ability?

- Is my eye on the goal, and am I living ready to hit it out of the park?

- Create a simple but doable action plan to grit out that difficult thing.

- Which area of my life would be better served if I choose to spit, grin, and go on?

_____

_____

_____

_____

_____

15

Bigger Beards and Bushy Brows

The more you reaffirm who you are in Christ, the more your behavior will begin to reflect your true identity.

—Neil T Anderson

The makeup of the '80s was fashionable in my era, but not necessarily my jam. Back in the day, extreme style, big hair, and pop culture was the thing, and more makeup was *more*—with bright full lipstick, neon-colored eye shadow, and bold bushy eyebrows. But then, the '90s hit, and it was all about the brows, the razor-thin, over-plucked brows.

Celebrities and teenage girls clamored to get rid of their full natural brow, preferring to pencil mini arches over their lids.

My sister wasn't immune to the allure of the 90's brow swerve. With a headful of thick silky hair that reached her waist and bushy eyebrows that draped her face, she was a perfect candidate for my cosmopolitan skills. Not to worry—I would take care of it. But would I take care?

After convincing my sister that this would be fast and easy—even painless—she agreed to my makeover offer. I sat her down in a comfy chair in front of the bathroom full-length mirror and set to work.

Plucking long, twiney, stubborn eyebrow hairs hurt. These were not the teeny tiny, barely-there type of hairs. She started to fidget, and I knew my time for making her beautiful was running out. So I shielded my next move from her by telling her if she kept her eyes closed, I wouldn't poke her eyeball. Then I reached inside the shower for my … wait for it. Shaver! Biting my lip ever so slightly, I lowered the shaver in an arched position to create the perfect brow. But as I was in motion, the bathroom door suddenly opened with a jerk, and so did my hand. One second I was meticulously trimming and the next, regretfully witnessing a deeply gouged brow. It was bleeding and would one day scar to retell the botched makeover story.

Finding a Deeper Beauty

I believe 2020 is a makeover story, a gouge of sorts, where something unforeseen impacted all of us in one way or another and took us to a deeper place. The year was predicted to be one of clear vision, and it definitely was an eye-opener for more than we ever could have imagined. Many of us saw deeper than the skin, in our own lives and in others. We saw the raw, ugly, and horrific. Scars in our history, marriages, and families resurfaced. They were disturbing, to say the least. Without a bunch of distractions, we were forced to deal with them.

Leading up to that time, we lived in style and in vogue, with bigger beards and fuller eyebrows, but were we truly in touch? — in touch with our spouse, in touch with our hurting neighbor, in touch with our kids, with our hidden feelings, and our heathen prejudices?

This awakening has brought forth a new period where we are aching and longing for true beauty that runs deeper than the surface — a beauty of the soul that lives fuller and loves deeper in a world full of hurt and hate. But how can we, planted upon this good green earth as faulty human beings, ever measure up to reaching such a beautiful level of spiritual maturity?

Often, we assume "new" to be perfect, stunning, and admirable. The word new appeals to us. A stand-alone item. An independent person. A thing ideal. An outward symbol of completion.

New living, thinking, and being isn't a surface thing. It is a deeper living that begins at the root, inside our hearts. Jesus spoke these words of continual nourishment to humans living their best life: "I am the vine, you are the branches. He who abides in Me, and I in him, bears much fruit; for without Me you can do *nothing*" (John 15:5 NKJV emphasis mine).

Abiding in Christ gives us the nutrients needed for successful living. "If you abide in me, and my words abide in you, ask whatever you wish, and it will be done for you" (John 15:7). Growing in Him gives us the abundant life of bearing fruit. "By this my Father is glorified, that you bear much fruit and so prove to be my disciples" (John 15:8).

Connect to the vine of Christ and gain your nutrition and soul-food from Him. Quit depending on complicated outside sources to complete you. We live in Jesus. Not in fashion. Not in social media. Not in busyness. We find security and maturity in Him and know that, ultimately, we do nothing without Him. Connecting and growing is a good thing, but what exactly does that involve?

The Power of Chopping

"Mom, have you done your eyebrows lately?" my eight-year-old asked me as we drove to a girl's luncheon. I felt cute and was ready for her compliment. I smiled. But before I could respond, she finished with, "Well, you need to."

Much like eyebrows, beards, and bushes, new living not only requires connecting to the vine, but it also requires upkeeping. I'm not a fan of overgrown brows, beards, or bushes. I don't grow a beard, so I can't say from personal experience, but I have waxed brows and trimmed bushes. Both take work. Managing them requires attention.

Why should we be surprised? We tend to steer our lives in the easiest and least resistant route. Like eyebrows that look fine, until they don't. Like beards that are untrimmed, hairy, and just … a nope. Our lives need to be trimmed of *things* that cause our spiritual conditions to become tangled—similar to wild, thorny vines that get out of hand, overgrowing the good and new. It's not uncommon for hedges to outgrow their shape. Once this occurs, gardeners must prune heavily to retrain them.

Picture a gorgeous nostalgic red brick church, capped with white cornerstones, a large arched stained-glass window centered in front, a black roof and white steeple touching the clouds above, and graced with lush green shrubbery below. Here in this lovely setting, my husband and I made one of the harshest gardening decisions—to drop the long-handled loppers and bring out the 'ole chain saw. A deciduous species had grown over 12 feet tall and was overtaking the other plants. Not only was it sucking up space and nutrients, but it also looked thick, stocky, and ugly. We wanted green, leafy, and healthy. Chopping the lowest heaviest branches back to the trunk forced the new growth to rely solely on the source.

What has God chopped out of your life lately? Does it still sting? In our spiritual garden, *No.thing* catches us off guard. But confirmation on healthy growth that comes only from healthy roots gives us the assurance to remain connected when we feel chopped. Let the cutting remind us that the roots of our dependence rely upon God as our sustenance and source. We are becoming stronger and healthier. I don't want to rely on myself. My strength is found in Christ alone. Without Him, we can do nothing.

Please don't misunderstand; I am not in any way talking about browbeating or berating yourself. Neither am I suggesting that God cuts us, hurts us, or makes mistakes while trimming off the excess. What I am describing is that necessary action which our loving Savior allows to help lift and remove the tangled mess we are wrapped up in. "The purpose of the pruning is to improve the quality of the roses, not to hurt the bush" —Florence Littauer.[1]

The virtue of *No.thing* is to remove, discard, or trim away miscellaneous activities that choke out spiritual health. What can we do?

- Revive our hearts by digging into the Scriptures that give us spiritual nutrients.

- Realign our goals and achievements by fasting, praying, and seeking God's ways.

- Redirect the sap of our time and energy to vigorously growing stems of meaningful and enduring purpose.

We are fresh and new. We've thrown off the hostage-holding habits of madly dashing forth in exhausting busy work, trying to get all the things done. Let's consider *No.thing* as a gift to accelerate our actions to become more purposeful in our 24/7 activities.

Here is where shaping comes to play.

A Purposeful Shaping

Jesus sees us as works-in-progress, both living as citizens of His kingdom and developing saints on earth who need repentance and discipline. Plants are much like people, living in a balance between the above ground and below ground. Plants need plenty of top greenery to support their growing root system; people require a stable grounding that holds them through the weathering of life. Our stability is found in our identity with Christ the vine. And our structure (Christian living) is sheared and shaped by Him.

This week, my ego got chopped. I manage properties and opened an email from one of the vendors we lease from, notifying me that our lot rates had increased and that we were $100 short on our payment. Although it means an extra $1,200 a year, it really wasn't the money that bothered me but the lack of communication and professionalism on their part, that I wasn't notified in advance of the rate increase. The email further demanded that a check be cut and mailed by the end of the week. This company had done the same thing two years ago, and I sent an email requesting that all correspondence be either mailed to our PO Box or emailed directly to me. I had been nice once. The inconsideration ticked me off.

I didn't want to hear this message of embracing the shaping. No, I wouldn't take it this time. Immediately, I sat down at my desk and fired off a curt response. But the gardener of my heart knew that type of outburst would choke out my joy and steal my love for others. Early the next morning, I was driving into town and listening to the audio Bible when I felt a check in my soul. It was as if Jesus, the gardener, was trying to show me a picture of our world as an overgrown garden of hurt, hate, anger, and bitterness.

I saw myself in that garden, criticizing everyone else for being hateful and blaming the world for being in a crazy mess. Yet my own attitude was contributing to the jumbled-up tangle. I'm a Christ-follower, yet my ego got out on the wild side. It had to be cut back with a sincere and humble apology. Our lives will either become shaped by the world or shaped by the Word.

Gardeners know that hedges and plants should be cut back. They need it. Shearing them encourages robust new growth and ensures that sunlight reaches all parts of the bush. Even the best gardeners will tell you that pruning doesn't end when hedges become mature and well-established. You get the picture—becoming new and remaining connected to Christ establishes consistent new growth in our lives. So how do we achieve or maximize that growth?

If you have ever tried to grow longer lashes or bought for someone sporting a bigger beard, you may have explored the topics of a more lucrative lash serum or a better beard balm. Whenever we are talking about our lives and our souls, it should seem natural, not odd, that self-care includes our relationship as branches connecting to the vine of Christ.

Neither should we be surprised if we require a cutting of some old habits and retraining of some old ways of thinking. Check your attitude. Maybe you aren't always right. Make genuine apologies. Adjust your words to your spouse. Listen to whatever God talks to you about as you read and pray. Don't shy away from the shearing and shaping.

Initially, you may feel a little odd or a bit uneven. It's okay. At first, trimmed hedges can turn out bald-stemmed and ugly in places, but soon new growth fills those areas, producing thicker, healthier, and more uniform than before. You are new and taking shape to produce wonderful fruit in your life. A healthy life. A better life. One free of thistles, weeds, and overgrown vines that threaten to choke you out.

Step back and watch yourself pull off that new style God is shaping on the outside of you!

(And, just in case you were wondering about my sister with the overgrown eyebrows, she still hasn't forgiven me for wrecking her brow line. I don't authorize or recommend shaving them. Stick with waxing or plucking).

Digging Deeper

- Am I more prone to be shaped by the world or the Word of God?

- In what area is Christ shaping or molding me?

- How open am I to receiving instruction and leadership from the Word?

- Do I respond quickly to the reshaping?

_____

_____

_____

_____

_____

_____

_____

Section Four

Know thing

/know/ verb
  1. *be aware of through observation, inquiry, or information.*

*I **know** that you can do anything and **nothing** that you plan is impossible. (Job 42:2 ISV, emphasis mine)*

16

Why Nothing?

Love is a Person Who wants to be known.

—Catherine Toon

Have you ever been embarrassed by your small children? When it comes to building us up, there's not a better feeling in the world than receiving their purest love and admiration. But kids have an uncanny way of being brutally honest. And as fast as they prop you up, it can all come crashing down in a hurry, and the mom ego rug is jerked right out from under us.

Our son was a compliant, cute little thing, and all the parishioners in our small congregation loved him. At the close of Sunday morning service, he would stand beside Jay and me as we greeted those leaving. Patiently, Markey stood every week waiting for "Mr. Candyman" to come by and slip a piece of candy inside their handshake. I could count on him to stand there politely without me having to fuss at him.

However, that Sunday, I got caught up in a conversation and Markey escaped to the other end of the room. Scanning the area, I noted one of the most distinguished deacons in our church bending over to say something to my small son, who was eagerly standing on tiptoes. As the man reached forward, his suit coat fell open slightly and then, in horror, I watched Mark's little arm outstretched as he grabbed and *snapped* the suspenders of this man, a.k.a., our local state representative. I rushed over and tried to correct the situation, but it got worse when I heard my son ask the rotund gentleman, "But, *why* do you wear those, anyway?"

Kids notice everything, and they aren't afraid to ask why. We need to know the secret sauce of Christianity, just like my son and the man dressed for success. We can't reprimand a kid who caught a glimpse of something he had never seen before. He didn't have an attitude, he just wanted to know.

We say things like, "It's not what you know, but who you know." Our secret to developing maturity is found in the know.

> *God is the link between our No.thing and our Know thing.*

The answer is not in a *thing* at all, but in a person—Jesus Christ. We need to know what God thinks by studying His words. We need to know how we should live by examining His life. We need to know how to apply what we know. Because it's true, you don't know what you don't know ... but until I know what I know about who I know—then and only then am I able to apply what I know about *Who* I know. And what I definitely know is that God is the link between our *No.thing* and our *Know thing*.

The ah-ha moment for me in writing this book and on this topic is found in the following paragraph. It both shakes me and challenges me. We've explored the reality of now, the insecurity of the next, and discovered identity in our new. But as we step deeper into the maturity of knowing, you need to know this: The greatest act of redemption was not the birth of Jesus or His death on the cross. His greatest act preceded these.

Did you know that the God of the entire universe humbled himself and became *no thing*? Philippians 2:5-8 cracks open my mind and heart: "Have the same mindset as Christ Jesus: Who, being in the very nature of God, did not consider equality with God something to be used to his own advantage; rather, he made himself *nothing* by taking the very nature of a servant, being made in human likeness. And being found in appearance as a man, he humbled himself by becoming obedient to death—even death on a cross" (emphasis mine).

Another translation says that He "emptied himself," which means that no one could do it for Him. Jesus Christ stripped Himself of honor, dignity, and majesty. He came to this earth as nothing but a micro millimeter of a seed planted inside of Mary's womb. Subjecting Himself for nine months to the sound of embryonic fluid, hearing the rush of blood as it circulated through His mother's body, and feeling the gentle rub of her hand through a thin wall of tissue that separated them.

Can you even fathom that the God who created this world took on the form of a human body by growing inside the uterus of a created being? In this fashion, Jesus was silent, small, unnoticed, and irrelevant to most of the world. Yet if you ever contemplated the anomaly of these events, here's the answer to the why question: Jesus believed in the plan of His Father and the purpose of redemption so much that He completely emptied Himself to become one of us. He chose to experience firsthand and to know what it meant to live in skin.

Leveraging Your Leverage

At first, *No.thing* might appear to be a negative, something to run from, yet Christ challenges us to know the answer by embracing humility and the power found inside it. The Son of God did not become a Savior without first becoming a servant. We have to know that Jesus Christ made Himself nothing, yet He was not intimidated or restricted by it. On the contrary, the advantage of *No.thing* leveraged Him into something greater. Humbling and dying meant living. This was an oxymoron on the surface, yet He purposely showed us what living in humanity and humility really looks like.

Our number one enemy, Satan, doesn't want us to get a full grasp of this greatest act toward the reconciliation of mankind (us) back to the Creator. Pride brought Lucifer down, sealing his eternal fate. To get revenge, he wrapped pride inside of a piece of fruit and tempted the first woman in the garden. It worked better than imagined. With the game over, the entire human race had no chance of redemption. But then Jesus humbled Himself to bring His children back home. He didn't have to. He wanted to. Knowing this brings me to my knees, and I have to keep coming back to this convicting message of humility. We've got to know the Father's heart when it comes to this act of *No.thing*. It's the core attraction of Christianity.

There's nothing more beautiful than a child who humbles himself on his own volition and admits that he needs you. The love a parent feels for a child in that moment is incredibly unfathomable, and there isn't a mountain we wouldn't move for that child.

My nephew and son are close to the same age. Their curiosity led them to adventures and beyond. I guess they were about two and a half when the "babies" raided the pantry and sneaked a large unopened can of blueberry lemonade under the bed with them.

My sister and I didn't notice they were gone at first. We just assumed they were in the playroom with the other kids. Things were too quiet. Where were they? We went on a child hunt. All through the house, outside around the pool, searching over and under everything. Finally, going back into the master bedroom, we heard not giggles y'all, but smacking little lips coming from under the bed—one that had a brand-new white comforter, sheets, and bed skirt on it and handprints marking the territory.

We bent over to find carpet and 20 little fingers covered in blue sugar. The entire can was empty. They had hit the jackpot! Without missing a beat, they crawled out from under the bed and hugged our legs like we had given them the entire moon. Their hands stuck to us as we lifted them up and carried them to the bathtub. I don't even remember punishing them because they were so delighted in the prize, and we were just grateful that we found them alive.

Do you ever wonder what gets into the head of a kid who really isn't trying to be bad? All they can see is fun, and their curiosity just gets the best of them.

Humbling doesn't mean that we are in trouble; it means that we are willing and vulnerable enough to be held. We want the assurance of having our Father's full attention, and we are curious enough to do whatever it takes to get it. "Humble yourselves in the sight of the Lord, and He will lift you up" (Jas. 4:10 NKJV).

Those curious to know more about Jesus need to know that living in humility starts to feel lighter and natural when we understand the benefits of *No.thing*. I'm a proud individual and humbling myself is a big deal (There! I said it). Yet the message of Christ compels me to know Him more and to keep falling in love with Him daily by following His pattern of humility.

No.thing seems to take the controls away from me, where there is nothing more I can manage or manipulate. In a sense, it's a good thing. It gives me permission to take my hands off whatever may be the *thing* at the time and causes me to surrender myself (again and again) to the will and ways of God. Humbling myself and releasing my own wishes and desires gives me a glimpse of the personal investment Jesus has made into my life. I then rest in the knowledge that He is in full control of my purpose and passions. I become dependent, like a child again, and I know He won't let me down.

His humbling went a step further. Not only did Christ model humility to His father by becoming a man in skin, but He took it to another level when He again humbled Himself as a man to become a servant. This! This is what He calls us to—a beautiful life of servanthood. To be like Christ, we have to live like Him. To love like Christ, we have to serve like Him. To be obedient like Christ, we will have to intentionally humble ourselves like He did.

Not many of us are willing to humble on our own. Generally, it takes adverse circumstances or a humbling experience to nudge us in that direction. But if we want to know Christ more deeply, we will need to be curious and gutsy enough to take the same path of humbling ourselves by daring to believe that less of us means more of Him. How you get there really doesn't matter, but we all need to get there somehow.

Digging Deeper

- How is what I know to be true about God bringing me to a season of maturity?

- Am I expecting growth in my spiritual life, and how can servanthood increase it?

- What *No.thing* has created a deeper hunger inside of me to know God more fully?

_____

_____

_____

_____

_____

_____

17

Not for Nothing

*Be anxious for **nothing**, but in everything by prayer and supplication, with thanksgiving, let your requests be made known to God.*

—Philippians 4:6 NKJV, emphasis mine

I rushed in the door and threw myself onto the bed, sobbing uncontrollably. My prayers had been crushed, not answered. I had faith, and now it was shaken to the core. What happened?

As a teenage girl, I was faced with one of the worst battles in my young Christian life. I had prayed a prayer I was sure God had heard. My friend would be healed from cancer. I knew without a doubt that God had spoken directly to me. Now, she was gone.

I tossed and turned fitfully as I wondered how a loving God could have lied and let me down—let her down. Despite the excruciating pain she suffered, she had been extremely brave. I remembered her smile and kind words to those who cared for her. A life that was a blessing to all was gone, leaving me utterly confused.

For weeks, I went through the motions of Christianity—reading my Bible, going to church, and praying. It was hopelessly stale and dry. I started wondering if I could really trust a God who said one thing and did another. When nothing good happened, I doubted Him and His promises. I began to feel like I didn't need a God like this, and slowly my heart became closed and my relationship with Him turned silent.

But He didn't let me go. As I sat alone in grief one day, God cracked the silence with these four words: I *did* heal her.

I twisted up my lips. "What? I don't understand, God. I prayed, and you got my hopes up. Then, you said *no!*"

The words were barely out of my mouth when a picture of my friend flashed before me. She was laughing, clapping, and dancing through heaven. "*She is completely healed,*" He then reassured me.

While her passing from this life was a *no* to my prayer, it was the *thing* that heaven had prepared just for her! Knowing this flipped the script for me. I needed to hear it then as a teenager, and I still need to know it today. It isn't all for nothing; my prayer is important. "We have to pray with our eyes on God, not on the difficulties" —Oswald Chambers.

> As maturing Christian believers, we have to know that our faith is firmly rooted in the Miracle Worker and not merely fixate on the miracle itself.

As maturing Christian believers, we have to know that our faith is firmly rooted in the Miracle Worker and not merely fixate on the miracle itself. Making demands on my expectations is not a mark of spirituality, nor is it the message Jesus teaches us. In maturity of faith, we petition our requests with thanksgiving for all God has done, and then we leave the miracle—whatever that may be—up to Him.

Traumatic Pandemic

"I feel like I've been sent off to war with nothing but a pocket-knife," my daughter, who is an RN, said to me on her way out the door—headed to a 12-hour shift on the COVID-19 floor. The reality of the coronavirus landing on our soil was colossal, especially with proceeding news reports of how quickly and brutally this virus attacked those across the ocean in other parts of the world.

In northern Louisiana, we knew we were in trouble when the virus started spreading like wildfire about three hours away in New Orleans. Like many hospitals, ours was unprepared for a pandemic of this magnitude. Overnight, my daughter's observation unit was turned into a restricted COVID-19 unit. The uncertainty and risks, along with not having the proper protection (PPE), was terrifying. Nurses were told they might have to revert to wearing bandanas, as the coveted N95 masks were scarce. I wasn't okay with this. I was mad. Asking my 25-year-old daughter to work and do her job was one thing, but to do it unprotected was a complete **No**! in my book. Why hadn't someone planned better for this? None of us had been "ready" for any of it (remember the toilet paper fiasco?).

I went into mother bear mode, pulling strings, sending emails, making calls to our state representative and anyone else who I thought could help. I was headed to the top and wouldn't stop until I got the PPE these nurses needed to protect themselves from exposure. Day after day, I tried lobbying all the people in positions that could move mountains, yet I found no tangible way to acquire the supplies.

Impacted by the uncertainty of the situation, I felt betrayed, trapped, ignored, and angry. Should I call the TV station? Stand out in front of the hospital with a cardboard sign? A thousand voices were in my head, but there was nothing more I could humanly do without jeopardizing my daughter's honor. She had taken an oath and chosen to give herself for the lives of others. The battle was not mine, and I could fix nothing.

During the second week of lockdown, in the middle of the night, God spoke to me. He asked if I was willing to drive over to the hospital and pray for the health care providers and the supplies they needed. Was I making this up? But what could it hurt? Through the pouring rain, I drove. I parked in a darkened lot across from the hospital and cried my eyes out, begging God to touch these sick patients and to send supplies to the providers. Yes, God was the answer, and my prayer was not unseen.

All of us who lived through the COVID-19 pandemic know what I'm talking about—the wild rush of internal emotions that swung violently from day to day. We had to learn how to be gentle with ourselves and patient with others. None of us were prepared for uncertainty, and the only thing that saved our sanity was knowing that our God was in total control—even during the uncontrollable.

In the middle of crises, some of us automatically shut down before we can muster the strength to rise, while others come out swinging from the get-go. However you process information and proceed with action, we all need to know that *No.thing* along our journey has taken God by surprise—not crisis, not cancer, not divorce, not bankruptcy, not even a pandemic.

Our God is not afraid of uncertainty because He knows all things. He is in total control of those who trust implicitly, and the results are completely up to Him. Knowing this takes the pressure off my own humanity and allows me to give grace to myself and to those around me.

In the case of not having enough PPE for my daughter, my working and badgering did nothing, but in the end, God used my prayers and did the impossible. Supplies were sent to these health care workers within a week through a third party, but in the meantime, I believe that God laid His protecting hand upon them when there was nothing else we could do.

Be assured. This section of your life isn't for nothing. Maybe the pain you have experienced won't bring back a loved one or renew health to a body with an incurable disease, but you have something worth giving. Your life is worth living. God sees good things coming from you. Each day is a gift. You have purpose.

Even if your circumstances seem like a *No.thing* at the moment and you don't understand what He is doing in this phase, leap confidently into the area of prayer by placing your faith in a Father who is kind and good. See what God can do with it. Obey. Do what you know. And then know it isn't for nothing—He's got you!

Digging Deeper

- What do I know God is currently doing inside of me?

- Where has confidently praying and believing affected change in my life?

- How can I trust that prayer is working when I don't see the results?

_____

_____

_____

_____

_____

18

Nothing Wasted

Never let a good crisis go to waste.

—Winston Churchill

I once heard an old-timer tell how his large family sustained life during hard times. They raised pigs and "ate everything but the squeal." Even the curly tail they used as a handle, attached to a slab of hind end, to grease the cast iron skillet.

My mother-in-law survived The Great Depression and fully knew the meaning of wasting nothing. Throwing away leftovers or outdated food was taboo. In her youth, Sunday dinner was served on the grounds, where leftovers sat out for hours covered by a sheet and eaten just before parishioners journeyed home. No one gave a second thought to the need for refrigeration or the idea of food safety as we do today.

I grew up in a completely different generation and culture. You can imagine my horror, one Saturday morning, as I watched her cut mold off the bacon before frying it for our breakfast. Isn't Aflatoxin a cancer-causing poison produced by certain fungi growing on food? This isn't cheese we are talking about. For goodness' sake, it's pork!

Our Lord Himself addressed food shortage more than once in His earthly ministry. He used it to leverage the work of greater good:

> Jesus soon saw a huge crowd of people coming to look for him. Turning to Philip, he asked, "Where can we buy bread to feed all these people?" He was testing Philip, for he already knew what he was going to do.
>
> Philip replied, "Even if we worked for months, we wouldn't have enough money to feed them!"
>
> Then Andrew, Simon Peter's brother, spoke up. "There's a young boy here with five barley loaves and two fish. But what good is that with this huge crowd?"
>
> "Tell everyone to sit down," Jesus said. So they all sat down on the grassy slopes. (The men alone numbered about 5,000.) Then Jesus took the loaves, gave thanks to God, and distributed them to the people. Afterward he did the same with the fish. And they all ate as much as they wanted.
>
> After everyone was full, Jesus told his disciples, "Now gather the leftovers, so that *nothing is wasted*." So they picked up the pieces and filled twelve baskets with scraps left by the people who had eaten from the five barley loaves. (John 6:5-13 NLT, emphasis mine)

Nothing is wasted speaks to the benevolent and conservative side of me, as I picture both the generosity and the frugality of Jesus in this story. What an experience of a lifetime to see the Master take five loaves and two fish. Bless. Break. Distribute. Satisfy. Here is Jesus, the Creator of the universe, who could have easily turned stones into bread, pulled bread from His pocket, or called a prepared feast down from heaven to fall simultaneously in perfect proportions and land squarely on the lap of each person present. Instead, He used what was there in front of Him, prepared and kneaded by human hands. The thought that Jesus needed someone's kneaded bread thrills me. But that is exactly what Jesus does. He takes my natural—your natural—and makes it supernatural.

I've researched more speculations than I ever imagined about this very familiar Bible story. There are enough articles on finding hidden meanings, unraveling mysteries, and deciphering symbols to make your head spin. Some scholars put significance in the type of barley bread, which was the first grain to be harvested and used in celebrations. Other commentators attempt to uncover the mystery of the 12 baskets and seek to answer whether the baskets represent 12 tribes of Israel, 12 patriarchs, or 12 disciples.

While there is validity to types, shadows, and numbers in the Bible, I just want to know about the scraps. The leftovers. Tell me—what happened to them? Did the little boy who shared his lunch possibly take more food home than he brought?

As a girl, I remember my single mother working and cleaning houses to put food on the table for us. At the time, we didn't know how poor we were and always trusted that our mom would provide. I longed for the novelty items in the grocery store. How I wished they would one day land in our shopping cart. But they didn't. And while I don't remember having many leftovers in the fridge, we never went hungry. So baskets full of broken leftover pieces intrigue me because Christ clearly states, and John records, "that nothing be wasted." I want to know the connection. How does this relate to you? To us?

I believe the miracle here represents four things: Food, Faith, Fortitude, and Fake.

Food

As we get deeper into this fish and bread story, I learn the significant application. I take inventory of myself by recognizing Philip's response to Jesus, "Even if we worked for months, we wouldn't have enough money to feed them" (John 6:7). Philip was the pragmatic disciple, and the dilemma was strictly a food issue to him. Dietitian was not on his resume, and he didn't feel the least bit obligated to supply lunch for these people. It was neither practical nor feasible to feed this large of a crowd.

Faith

Philip recognized the food shortage, but the Scripture tells us that Jesus was testing Philip's faith: "For He (Jesus) already knew what He was going to do." *No.thing* will test our faith. We can't let it mess with what we know in our heads. A food crisis is a distraction. The disciples tended to forget that with Jesus, the big picture was never about the temporal, but the eternal. Jesus can handle a food situation, but having faith and fortitude to overcome a *No.thing* in our lives takes courage on our part. Ownership. Partnership.

Fortitude

The disciples had come to this area to be alone, to have some "me time" with the Master. They were tired of crowds and burnt out with serving. Weary. Done. People. Go. Home. Have you ever been in a place where it becomes only about serving the people, and you lose sight of the true calling—of serving Christ? When you have given and have nothing humanly left to give? Yet Christ wants us to know that He came to serve. When we serve beside Him, He does the heavy lifting of multiplying the resources. He is the one who gives us courage and strength amid pain or adversity. Our scraps of service do not go to waste.

Fake

The illustrated account gets personal in the next few verses by hitting the very core of *No.thing*, as we discover another underlying reason why *No.thing* bothers us so much. Performance must be a universal matter, and we see it portrayed in the following verses. The very next day, after the miracle of feeding the multitude happened, this same crowd gathered around and asked Jesus:

> "We want to perform God's works, too. What should we do?"
>
> Jesus told them, "This is the only work God wants from you: Believe in the one he has sent.... I am the bread of life." (John 6:28-29, 35 NLT)

This passage calls for me to respond. Am I a follower of Christ to perform, or am I committed to practice? Am I only taken up with the blessings, or do I also believe when it gets tough? Am I devoted to loving when I don't feel like loving, giving when it's not easy? Sticking in there when it gets rough?

I like to call it practice because biblical Christianity is practical—a life of personal development while daily putting the Scriptures to practice in my walk with Jesus. It's when I am devoted to the regimen of practicing my faith over and over again, knowing that nothing I commit to the kingdom of Christ is wasted. I'm not interested in becoming fake and merely performing Christianity. Performing is for the crowds. Practice is for *me*.

Going Lighter

Until she had children, my friend Mo had no interest in sports, exercise, or fitness of any sort. Post-maternity, everything changed. For the first time, Mo realized that if she wanted to get her body back, she would have to practice putting in some effort.

She started drinking more water, exercising, and found a coach that encouraged her on a fitness journey. The phrase "if we want change, we have to make a change" keeps her motivated. And she knows habits will either make or break her health goals.

Now, as a certified coach and trainer, she is helping others to create sustainable habits to practice daily, no matter where they are. "Less can definitely be more if you utilize what you have," she said while rubbing her arms and describing how sore she was from the online class she taught during the pandemic. The true benefit? Gym members were able to work out from home with nothing but a backpack! She followed up by saying, "Getting healthy doesn't mean that you need a bunch of extra stuff. There is so much we can do with just our bodies. People get hung up on fancy equipment and gyms, but all you need to get a solid workout is your own body weight. That's it! The truth is, we just need to move."

Practicing good habits to strengthen and increase your spiritual health takes finding what works for you. Praying at night may work better than getting up early in the morning. Reading your Bible on the YouVersion app might be beneficial. You may find it more convenient to listen to the dramatized audio Bible as you rock the baby, walk around the block, or drive to work. Know that seasons of life change, and there isn't a right or wrong way to grow spiritually. Don't get hung up on how you spend time with Jesus. Just do it. Your time with Him isn't wasted.

I first met my husband in high school, and we became friends. He then asked if he could call me, and we began to build a deeper friendship by sharing more personal things. We dated four years and spent more time together ice skating on the pond, going out to eat, and playing ping pong and chess. It wasn't what we were *doing* as much as it was the *being* that really mattered. We were not acting our way into a relationship. We were building a relationship!

After we married and the first baby arrived, things changed. While our precious time together was limited, I never traded *being* a wife for merely *acting* like a wife. Our relationship was too important, and we creatively found a way to value our sweet moments as a couple. Performance-based marriage doesn't work, and neither does performance-based religion.

Are you following me? Eternal merit is found in *being* not in *acting*. Being with Christ is never wasted; acting like I am, is.

We have to know that performing is just another tactic the enemy throws our way, luring us back into an egotistical position of having a *thing* to prove our validity and Christianity. It weighs me down when I get caught up in performing. And in the end, when performance doesn't produce the expected results, I feel deserted and left standing with nothing but a basket full of wasted good intentions.

This is where our resolve is put to the test—living daily for Jesus. Will I serve or will I withdraw? Perform or practice? Have the faith and fortitude to carry on:

- When the marriage doesn't turn out the way I thought it would.

- When the ministry seems disenfranchised and somewhat disconnected.

- When relationships and promises are broken.

- When performance doesn't measure up and practice falls short.

- When you feel like you wasted a season, missed a calling, or an opportunity.

I don't know where you are in your season of life or cycle of maturity, but I want to assure you that with Jesus, nothing given in His name is wasted. This is the weightier truth found in the story of feeding the 5,000—the bread representing eternal life is found in Jesus! *He* is the Bread of Life who gives us spiritual nutrition, life, and growth. We have to know that nothing of eternal value is wasted.

- Know that every tear is remembered.

  "You have collected all my tears in your bottle. You have recorded each one in your book." (Ps. 56:8 NLT)

- Know that your prayers are not wasted.

  "For the eyes of the Lord are on the righteous and his ears are attentive to their prayer." (1 Pet. 3:12)

- Know that every kind deed is rewarded.

  "If anyone gives even a cup of cold water to one of these little ones who is my disciple, truly I tell you, that person will certainly not lose their reward." (Matt. 10:42 NIV)

- Know that your faith is not wasted.

  "Truly I tell you, if you have faith as small as a mustard seed, you can say to this mountain, 'Move from here to there,' and it will move. Nothing will be impossible for you." (Matt. 17:20 NIV)

The gathering of the pieces in these stories reminds us to hang on to the miracles God has done in our lives. By recalling His provisions, we can know that He always provides. *No thing* in the kingdom of God is lost, and nothing is wasted. So we get back up when we are knocked down, knowing with full assurance that we can make it!

I've found that Jesus handles *No.thing* with mastery. I like to imagine Him staring nothing down and commanding, "Here is how we are going to deal with you. We will limit nothing, we will fear nothing, and we will waste nothing."

This same Jesus is calling out to us today, encouraging us onward, not to perform but to practice, challenging us to consistently live a life of serving Christ with faith and fortitude. Continue to commit your works to the LORD (Prov. 16:3). Your actions may seem to go unnoticed by others, but absolutely nothing given to His kingdom is wasted. Not one message preached or Sunday school lesson taught. Not one Bible study attended or one book written. Not one encouraging word spoken or one text sent. Not one child taken in or one cup of cold water given. Nothing done in His name will be wasted!

Today, be encouraged. Take a new look at what seems like pieces scattered along the pathway of life. They are more than breadcrumbs. Renew your spirit, practice your new walk, and know that God is a master at performing miracles with nothing but scraps given to Him!

Digging Deeper

- How has performing externally gotten me off track from practicing inwardly?

- How has disappointment distracted me?

- Where have I felt purpose in serving?

- Have I committed to my faith and actively passed it on to future generations?

_____

_____

Nothing

_____

_____

_____

_____

19

A Bigger Small

God's love is meteoric,
his loyalty astronomic,
His purpose titanic,
his verdicts oceanic.
Yet in his largeness
nothing *gets lost;*
Not a man, not a mouse,
slips through the cracks.

—Psalm 36:5-6 MSG, emphasis mine

I fell for a mean dare once by agreeing to ride one of the world's tallest wooden roller coasters, the legendary Texas Giant. Before I could change my mind, I was strapped in and we were moving. The sign at the top of the track read, "Wait! Let's discuss this," but it was too late. I couldn't get off. With heart pounding and head whirling, my body felt like it was in a hot buzzing cannonball as the coaster rattled thunderously down the track.

I have heard that the engineering of a wooden track can allow it to sway up to three feet with the tremendous force of energy. I can verify that when you are on it, a wooden roller coaster sounds dangerous and *feels* dangerous. It was terrifying!

Along the route were flags—I had previously planned to count all six of them as we flew by, but I only saw two before my eyes squeezed shut and stayed shut. I thought I was dying.

There is a comparison between wooden roller coasters and conventional steel coasters. I've been told that wooden ones are much spookier and bumpier. I wouldn't know for sure because that was my one and only coaster ride. Go ahead, you can argue smooth or bumpy all you want, but I will *never* settle for that type of *fun* again.

Smooth: bumpy. Large: small. Happy: sad. Young: old. Birth: death. The process of linear thinking is narrow, with one path toward completion while ignoring outside possibilities and alternatives. The corporate world of our western culture is built primarily upon linear critical thinking—i.e., *it works this way, and it can only work this way.*[1]

We didn't always process life this way. As children, we naturally gravitate to a more creative type of thinking using the right side of the brain. But at an early age, creativity is often stifled in school. From start to finish, kids are placed into grades according to their age, assigned to learning tracks of conformity, and then pushed to pursue the established end goal.

Humans learn to live by comparisons and evaluations. We make our decisions by classifying situations and factoring through a mental filter as either rich or poor, cloudy or sunny, big or small, yes or no. Linear thinking of *either/or* is normal and rational for us. Yet God wants us to know that He is a *both/and* type of thinker.

For example, what we would consider as two separate items—salt or pepper, right shoe or left shoe—God would view as one whole *set*. Another example would be the fundamentals of the water cycle: evaporation, condensation, and precipitation—all separate yet working together as a complete system. While we see *either* good things *or* bad things happening in our lives, God sees *"all* things working *together* for good" (Rom. 8:28 emphasis mine).

God is writing a series, not just a novel, and our lives are a critical part of that story. He takes every word and uses every punctuation mark to complete history. Therefore, God insists on working both in the big and in the small. Within the complexity of a large universe, we matter to Him. What appears big to us is small to Him, and what is small in our eyes is huge to God.

In the previous chapters, we have seen that a *no thing* is not intimidating to God. He isn't afraid of small things—using them or being present inside of them. Here's more proof. For nine months, Jesus was silent, small, unnoticed, and irrelevant to most of the world, yet in the capsule of a woman's womb developed the Savior of the entire world. Our finite minds can't grasp the largeness of God's plan that is a time continuum, planned before the beginning of this world. At creation, the entire world was formed with nothing but the spoken word—such a small action, but what a large production.

When my kids were younger, I remember them begging me to buy these tiny, colorful caplets. It seemed they could easily be swallowed by a five-year-old kid. If it worked and grew like they said, trying to remove a life-size mammal from my kid's stomach could be disastrous. I was skeptical of the packaging that promised, *get it wet and a dinosaur as big as Texas will appear*. All I needed was a bathtub full of water and bubbles. Say no more. A clean kid is worth the money. I am all about a bigger reward for a smaller payout. A three-dollar toy and a good reason for a bath was a win-win in my mind.

But God's mastery of bigger-small is much more than a magic trick He plays in science. His omnipotence of great power was compacted into this tiny child born in Bethlehem. In a big but small way, this child entered the world, and He grew. "Jesus grew in wisdom and stature, and in favor with God and man" (Luke 2:52 NIV). He was the richest man alive but became poor. "You know the generous grace of our Lord Jesus Christ. Though he was rich, yet for your sakes he became poor, so that by his poverty he could make you rich" (2 Cor. 8:9). He was of the highest authority, the most intelligent, and altogether worthy. Yet he humbled himself and made himself of no reputation (Phil. 2:7).

Throughout the history of mankind, we see God weaving an intricate pattern of small threads on a large tapestry of time. In an earlier chapter, we studied Abraham's life of obedience as he took his promised son up to Mount Moriah for sacrifice, where a lamb was found and offered in his place. This true account foreshadowed the sending of God's Son, Jesus, which directly affects us today. "For God so loved the world, that he gave His only begotten Son, that whosoever believeth on him should not perish, but have eternal life" (John 3:16 KJV). One man's death was efficacious enough to save the entire world.

We fit inside of His small:big, imperfect:perfect plan. Everything God does has a purpose. His purpose for us hasn't been lost in the shuffle of humanity. "In his largeness *nothing* gets lost; not a man, not a mouse"(Ps. 36:6, emphasis mine). His love hasn't gotten lost in a world full of hate. The *thing* He is doing inside us hasn't been lost with a *no* or *wait*. God doesn't lose His way, lose His train of thought, lose His cool, lose His mind, lose His confidence, or lose track of His kids. God does not lose! He hasn't lost me, and He hasn't lost you. Whether it is big or small, don't settle for anything less than His perfect will for you.

Living for Jesus is not a zero-sum game of ping pong or chess, where one person wins and the counterparty loses. Life is more than matching pennies or a tic-tac-toe game that dictates a win-loss.

The ride of your life might feel crummy and bumpy at times, but I promise you won't fall through the cracks. Keep your eyes open. Count the flags of His faithfulness. I guarantee you there

are way more than six! God is paving the way inch by inch for a lifetime of incredibly big things. Know this. Wait and see!

Digging Deeper

- When life gets uncertain, how often do I recall the goodness of God?

- What part of Psalm 36:5-6 speaks the loudest to me?

- How important is it to know that God sees me and knows right where I am?

_____

_____

_____

_____

_____

_____

_____

20

All or Nothing

Security is mostly a superstition. Life is either a daring adventure or nothing.

—Helen Keller

It was mother–daughter swim night, and I stood 20 feet in the air on the diving board at our downtown YMCA over an Olympic-sized pool. Adrenaline jolted through my body and throttled my legs as I jumped on the end of the long, white board and felt it spring under my feet. I had planned for this moment, waited my turn in line, and gotten up the nerve—I would dive tonight!

Below, my swim instructor called out, "Come on, you can do it!"

I balked momentarily and gazed down past her brown legs, treading bluish-colored water. Way down, at the bottom of the pool, I spotted a huge white cylinder that seemed big enough to swallow a 10-year-old girl. Immediately, questions like, "Can a pool drain kill you, and will I be sucked into it?" flooded my head.

"Let's go. I'm ready," my coach repeated.

"Do you promise to catch me if I go too far down?" I asked.

"Yes, I've got you," she said.

I knew I could trust my swim coach. She was strong, confident, and completely able to get me back up to safety. But in *my* head, I saw sharks, and the chlorine water began to smell a lot like saltwater. I pictured a giant vortex of spinning water sucking children down a drain and pumping them out into the Pacific Ocean. I could drown and be lost at sea forever! An overactive imagination, you might say, but my fear of the water separated me from leaping and enjoying the plunge into the deep that night.

Throughout this book, we have learned that a *thing* doesn't define us, label us, crush us, or stop us from finding our passion and purpose. We have addressed *No.thing* by combating our uncertainty in the now, establishing security while stepping into the next, breaking free and embracing our new identity, and, finally, by knowing the joy of developing spiritual maturity.

Implementing the four sections provides these four essential keys to leaping into God's everything:

- *Now* – Staying in tune, hearing God's voice, and walking to His beat

- *Next* – Shifting our thoughts and reframing our reality

- *New* – Breaking free of the old me and living free in a new identity.

- *Know* – Humbling myself, hungering for more of God by seeking Him and not a "thing" for fulfillment

When our kids were younger, we took a trip to the east coast to visit the Statue of Liberty and the sites of The Big Apple. Before starting out on our adventure, we went over all the safety precautions and put the buddy system into place. Our oldest was 16 at the time and had a fairly good head on her shoulders, so I wasn't concerned about her. And I had no worries over our 12-year-old son, busy navigating the entire trip with his phone app set to follow the NYC subway routes. But I had a death grip on the 5-year-old, who was flighty as a butterfly and light as a feather. She could easily be lost in New York City!

Our sightseeing took us across streets buzzing with traffic, overcrowded sidewalks, and down bustling subways. Having over 400 stations and countless lines, New York City has one of the largest transit systems in the world. With yellow lines, blue lines, purple and green lines, like ant tunnels weaving throughout this metropolitan city. At the corner of Times Square and 42nd, we quickly boarded the train. The doors closed, and like a dart, we shot off.

With my hand still clasping our youngest child, I glanced out the window to see our son standing alone on the curb with a helpless look in his eye as we flew past him. In the shuffle, we had been separated. Desperately, my husband yanked at the door, as if to force it open. But it wouldn't budge. "You've got to go back and get my son!" he yelled.

We had taken it for granted that our son had a phone and that he could communicate if we were separated, but there's no cell service underground in a subway station. None. My heart stopped and my head spun as the fear of losing a child in this maze came to reality. How could we have been so careless?

We were separated.

Separation brings fear, and fear brings separation. Satan realizes that when I am isolated, I become easy prey and the win is in his hand. But with confidence, we can *know* that *No.thing* can separate us from our loving Heavenly Father.

> Can anything ever separate us from Christ's love?
> Does it mean he no longer loves us if we have trouble
> or calamity, or are persecuted, or hungry, or desti-

tute, or in danger, or threatened with death? No, despite all these things, overwhelming victory is ours
through Christ, who loved us.

And I am convinced that *nothing* can ever separate us from God's love. Neither death nor life, neither angels nor demons, neither our fears for today
nor our worries about tomorrow—not even the pow-
ers of hell can separate us from God's love. No power
in the sky above or in the earth below—indeed, *nothing* in all creation will ever be able to separate us
from the love of God that is revealed in Christ Jesus
our Lord. (Rom. 8:35,37-39 NLT, emphasis mine)

From the moment that train took off from the station, heading away from our son, my heart, my head, and my prayers went
into action. With no other solution, we would have to get off this
train and board the returning train to go back and get him. I had
unanswered questions. What would he do? Would he wait for us
to come back, or hop a train and come looking for us?

As our train pulled into the station, we jumped off and
bolted to where we had left him. My daughter spotted his blue
shirt in a group of people getting on to the next shuttle heading
in the opposite direction. She lunged forward and shouted at the
top of her voice across the chasm between us. Miraculously, over
the chaotic clatter, Mark heard the voice and was stopped mid-
step from getting on the wrong train.

True, by all physical appearances, we had left him, but we
hadn't *left* him—we were coming back!

I want you to deeply know that whatever stage or cycle of
life you are in—you've got this, friend … and He's got *you*!

Keep looking for His hand to move, listening for His voice
and trusting in a God who hasn't left you alone.

God's love holds you and me—not a single thing can come
between us today! Not rejection. Not an election. Not a failed

business or failed marriage. Not racism or sexism. Not a promotion or demotion. Not hell or high water. No storm. No rival. No loss. No bad news. Neither life nor death can separate us from God.

Dare to declare this to a hurting world. Let's arise, naked before Him. Emboldened afresh and anew by believing and leaping into God's everything. Knowing without a doubt that not a thing stands between us and our Savior.

Absolutely *No.thing* separates us from God's love and purpose!

Afterword

As I was writing chapter five, "The Divine Fermata," news reached us that our daughter's condition may have relapsed, as they found a "spot" on her brain stem. I sat staring at this manuscript, re-reading these very words to myself. The events have given me whiplash, and the temptation is to ruminate on all the memories of that nightmare 15 years ago.

My former self would have immediately been sick in the pit of my stomach. My shoulders would have tensed up and my head would have raced. My nights would have been filled with fear and worry. But this time, by God's grace, it is different. I stop-checked my thoughts of denial and panic by putting into practice the strategies I have shared with you in this book. While I never expected to be here again and didn't expect to re-live them. I'm here to tell you on a personal, *now thing*, level—it works!

We fully believed that God healed Melissa from the brain tumor she experienced in 2005. For the last 15 years, there has been no sign of optic nerve damage or any other indication of extended or extenuating medical complications. Then recently, she started experiencing migraine headaches. The doctor ordered an MRI to clarify the issue. She ended up doing two more MRIs to clearly identify the image.

It felt like deja vu. I just stood there as the prognosis came back: "It may be a tumor, fluid, or MS. We found a spot on her stem cell and have made a consult to the neurosurgeon."

How could this be happening again? I recalled the time when, as a little girl, Melissa felt God calling her to nursing. She fulfilled that call by working as an RN for the past three years.

Having just started classes this fall to pursue her master's as a nurse practitioner, she confessed, "Mom, this news all came at the wrong time. I don't have time for this." The exact words I had said when she was 10 years old and diagnosed with a brain tumor.

None of us have time for pain and suffering. It's never a good time for adversity, and waiting is dreaded when we want the diagnosis, prognosis, and questions answered now. Most of us seek solutions and immediate fixes because we desperately want to skip the middle. But in our hearts, we know that all things work together for our good within the process. And while waiting for an answer can be harder than a *no*, it is in the pause that God is writing His greater story.

I'm in it here with you, right now, as the clock ticks along with my keyboard. I, too, am waiting … waiting for an answer from the neurosurgeon. It's here, in the middle of the "no" and the "thing" that I pause with expectation, believing that this pain, setback, wait, is once again molding me into who God wants me to be. Not only is it growing me, but it is giving my now-adult daughter the opportunity to rise above the obvious and to expect the miraculous. It's not the end. We are in the middle. Today, God is writing our story in the now. Present tense. We choose to believe now for our next, new, and *know* that His ways and thoughts are much higher than ours (Isa. 55).

I'm saying this to you, to me, and to her—don't be afraid of the dots and the swats. It's working for our good.

Melissa believes her life is in God's hands. He has given her assurance that she is healed, even though the spot still shows on the screen. She is grateful to be functioning at a high level with minimal headaches and going full force into travel nursing while doing clinicals and finishing her FNP degree.

UPDATE: As I put the final edits in on this book, the doctor has confirmed that the spot is not growing and appears asymptomatic. I am relieved and grateful. We know God has great things planned for our daughter's next thing and her new thing. I'm saying this to you, to me, and to her—don't be afraid of the dots and the swats. It's working for our good. Nothing is wasted, and we ain't seen nothing yet, so keep gritting, spitting, and grinning!

Notes

Chapter 1 | Now What?

[1] Collins, J. (2017). *The Stockdale Paradox*.

https://www.jimcollins.com/media_topics/TheStockdaleParadox.html

Collins, J. (2001). *Good to Great*. Harper Collins Publisher.

Chapter 6 | The Shift

[1] Reagan, J. Blue Bloods (2012) Season 2, Episode 17: "No Questions Asked." tvfanatic.com.

Chapter 7 | Reframe and Rename

[1] *Atlanta Magazine*, April 2008. https://priverevaux.com/products/the-mlk, MLK exhibit at Atlanta Airport (2009). https://stuckattheairport.com/2009/01/19/mlk-exhibit-at-atlanta-airport/.

[2] Leaf, C. (2019, September 20). How to Stop Toxic Thinking Episode #96 podcast. http://podcast.drleaf.com/e/episode-96-the-influence-ofgeneticshow-to-stop-toxic-thinking-how-to-formhealthy-habitsthebeauty-offailure-and-more-interview-on-themelanie-avalonbioh/; Leaf, C. Cleaning Up the Mental Mess. https://anchor.fm/cleaningupthementalmess

[3] Grant, A. Twitter post from Feb 11, 2014.

Chapter 8 | Pull Out the Cotton Balls

[1] Horowitz, S. (2012). *The Universal Sense: How Hearing Shapes the Mind* (1st ed.). Bloomsbury USA.

[2] Carey, Mariah https://gothamist.com/arts-entertainment/mariah-carey-is-mortified-about-her-horrible-new-years-eve, https://www.tmz.com/2017/01/01/mariah-carey-new-years-eve-performance-sabotage-emotion/, https://ew.com/tv/2017/01/02/mariah-carey-nye-what-really-happened/

[3] Murphey, Kate (Jan 2020). You're Not Listening: What You're Missing and Why It Matters. Published by Celadon Books.

Chapter 9 | Set Down Your Water Pot

[1] Eldredge, Stasi (Sept 2014). *Becoming Myself: Embracing God's Dream of You.* David C Cook; New, Trade Paperback edition.

Chapter 11 | Breaking Free

[1] Mangone, R. D. (2019). *Busted: A Banker's Run to Prison.* Published by Bezalel Prison Ministries.

Christianity Today. (2020, February 6). "My Name Was on a Federal Most-Wanted List. Now It's Written in the Book of Life." https://www.christianitytoday.com/ct/2020/february-web-only/richard-mangone-busted-banker-run-prison.html.

[2] Braby, M. F. (2018, August 27). Curious Kids: Do butterflies remember being caterpillars? *The Conversation.*https://theconversation.com/amp/curious-kid-do-butterflies-remember-being-caterpillars-99508

Notes

Chapter 15 | Bigger Beards and Bushy Brows

[1] Florence Littauer (2001). "It Takes So Little to Be Above Average," Harvest House Pub

Chapter 19 | A Bigger Small

[1] Miker, S. (2020). Linear Thinking Versus Systems Thinking. Scott Miker. https://www.scottmiker.com/linear-thinking-versus-systems-thinking.

Author of *You Can't Surf from the Shore and Turn Potential into Production.*